## That Reminds Me

## Ship Yard & Tug Boat Stories

By Robert (Bob) Mattsson

Text Copyright © 2014 Robert Mattsson

All Rights Reserved

ISBN-13: 978-1499629828

ISBN-10: 1499629826

# Dedication

This book is dedicated to my beautiful wife Gail who put up with me being away from home having fun as described in these tales while she was bringing up my son Shawn and running a household. And also while ignoring her while writing and rewriting these stories on the computer.

# Introduction

As a member of the group, tugboats@yahoo.com I would begin following a thread on the emails and there were things in that thread that would jog my memory about my younger days in the ship yard and on the tugs. I would relate these memories to the group and after awhile there were quite a few of these stories and my cyber friends insisted I write a book about my experiences. These stories cover about 10 years of my early employment from my time in the ship yard to becoming an oiler and finally an engineer before I went ashore and into management. And a few stories from my ship yard management time. I hope you enjoy them.

## Table of Contents

Dedication
Introduction
Chapter 1 The Beginnings
Chapter 2 - Black Tom Yard
Chapter 3 - Tug & Barge Yard
Chapter 4 - Typical Day
Chapter 5 - Cranes
Chapter - 6 Labor Gang
Chapter - 7 Electricians Gang
Chapter - 8 Trying to Break In
Chapter - 9 Alignment
Chapter 10 My Big Break
Chapter 11 - Ellen F. McAllister
Chapter 12- Dry Docks
Chapter 13 - Jersey Central Ferries
Chapter 14 - Wheel Gang
Chapter 15 - Asbestos
Chapter 16 - Stern Bearings
Chapter - 17 Wm. H. McAllister
Chapter 18 - Eileen McAllister
Chapter 19 - The Three Copper Cigars
Chapter 20 - Steering on the Hudson
Chapter 21 - Winter Watchman
Chapter 22 - Margaret McAllister
Chapter 23 - Appendicitis
Chapter 24 - Birthday and Payback
Chapter 25 - Painting the Engine Room

Chapter 26 - Peter B. McAllister

Chapter 27 - The Firing Range

Chapter 28 - NYS Barge Canal Things

Chapter 29 - Cockroaches

Chapter 30 - Shifting At Brooklyn Piers

Chapter 31 - Runaway Tug

Chapter 32 - Some Other Stories

Chapter 33 - Stranded on Ice Flows

Chapter 34 - Christine E. Fire

About the Author

# Chapter 1 The Beginnings

I was born Robert Mattsson on November 6, 1939, on Staten Island, New York. My nick name when I was young was 'Matty', but as I got older everyone just called me 'Bob'. I had 6 siblings, Gertrude (Trudy), Arne (Motsy), who were older than me. Younger than me were Melvyn and Maureen who were twins, Carl and then Bruce who came after the twins. My mother Cecilia was from Ireland and my father Arne was born in Norway. They met in Brooklyn, N.Y., got married and moved to Staten Island, New York where we were all raised. I went to grade school from kindergarten to 8th grade at P.S 29 and from there to Curtis High School near Saint George on Staten Island, New York.

    All the boys ended up in the marine industry. Arne became a captain on a New York City Police Boat after working on the tugs for awhile and retired from the Police Department after 25 years, then he became a plant supervisor for Royal Petroleum. Mel became a chief engineer on the tugs for McAllister, then Eklof which became K-Sea and is now Kirby Offshore. Mel was still at it as of 2014. Carl was a whiz of an electrician in the shipyard before he also went on the tugs as a chief engineer, first for McAllister and then for Eklof. He quickly became a port engineer for Eklof and designed and built automation for a few of their tugs and tankers. Carl became sick with throat cancer and passed away at a relatively young age. Bruce, the youngest also became a tug engineer and retired in 2013 as the senior chief engineer for Great Lakes Towing. Bruce is now writing books to help engineers in their day to day operations and to help with their USCG exams.

Robert Mattsson

Around 1947, when I was eight or nine years old, I began begging my father, Arne, to take me to work with him. He was an engineer on steam tugs for McAllister Towing company at the time. The answer was always no, but I found out that answer was actually coming from my mother, Cecilia, and so I changed tactics. Begging incessantly for days on end I finally wore her down and I got the okay. We rarely saw my father in the morning as he left the house at about 5:00 am. So when he said I could go with him and that I should go to bed early, I tried but I could hardly sleep for the anticipation. He woke me at 4:30 am and we were off by 4:50. The trip from Staten Island to Jersey City was just over a half hour and when we reached the rail yard it was still dark. After parking we walked down the tracks and across the float bridge to a car float and then onboard the tug. It was chilly but I could care less. The tug was either the J.P McAllister or the Isabel McAllister or the G.M. McAllister, he had been engineer on all three. The picture of the three tugs tied up in the East River comes from the *Steven Lang Maritime Collection*. The tug was steady on this job moving railroad car floats from Jersey City to Brooklyn and back. The crew coming on was busy exchanging information with the crew getting off and I was told to sit on the settee in the engine room and not to move. I could see the railcars moving on the car float through a port light and the Dutch door of the engine room. I couldn't see the whole railcar as we were right alongside and they looked gigantic to me. I watched the wheels on the rail car trucks

as they went squealing by with wide eyes. The smell of steam, oil and smoke made things even more exciting. Occasionally the air was refreshed by a cool morning breeze coming through from the Dutch door on the other side of the engine room. It was relatively quiet in the upper engine room and that surprised me. There was a small turbine generator running and down below one or two boiler furnace blowers, although at the time I had no idea what they were. The crew change over, my father brought me to the galley where we ate a monstrous breakfast while the car float was being reloaded. I was introduced to the crew who all looked big, gruff and frightening to me but treated me very nice and would tousle my hair as they went by and make some remark about going to school or saving my money. In the engine room I was introduced to the fireman and the oiler. The fireman was from Spain, the oiler was from Greece, my father was from Norway and I was from Staten Island, NY and here we all were in Jersey City, NJ.

    Back in the engine room a jingle of the cow bell above the control stand indicated the car float and the captain were ready to go. My father hit the cow bell with his hand to signal back that he was ready. There was a cover over half the large gong bell and near the cowbell that was attached to 1 ½" brass tubes that carried the sound back to the pilothouse so the captain knew the signal was sent. A change in speed or direction told him it was received and acted on. There was a flurry of bells and jingles as we got underway and my father was pushing and pulling levers to make the triple expansion steam engine do what was required so the captain could maneuver and get out into the harbor. Once we were underway the bells stopped and my father called the oiler to the control stand and took me to the lower engine room to show me the underside of the steam engine. From the upper engine room all you could see was the large flat heads of the cylinders and the black sheet metal covering the insulation on the cylinder sides. From below it was an entirely different story; the piston rods were pumping up and down with the connecting rods following in their crosshead slides with the bottom ends connected to the spinning crankshaft. Besides this were the cylinder valve linkages all moving and the large flywheel spinning. It was amazing to watch. We walked over to the boilers where the fireman was watching the air draft, the fuel nozzles, the fuel temperature and the shape of the fire in the firebox through the little mica windows. By regulating the air and fuel he would keep the steam pressure near a constant pressure when running at full speed or while maneuvering when less steam was required. After a while my father could see I was tired so he showed me his room and asked if I wanted to lie down. I did and climbed in the bunk (I thought *that* was real neat) and went to sleep immediately. They woke me at lunch time. Another big meal and then I was brought up to the pilothouse and told to sit on a stool behind the captain. I watched for awhile, my father came up, saw I was sleepy again and let me go to his room and go to sleep again. He woke me when it was almost time to get off. So my friends, that was my first tugboat experience. I loved it and never forgot it. I think, even at that young age that I was impressed with how independent each and every crew member was. No one really had a boss and yet everyone was doing their job and seemed to like what they were doing. It made a big impression on me.

Originally on steam boats you had, beside the engineer, an oiler, wiper and fireman. Oil fired was easier than coal fired, the fireman could take care of the boiler more or less by himself. The oiler and wiper would lend a hand to each other and the engineer when needed. Coal boats were a lot harder and the oiler and wiper had to chip in to pass coal and feed the firebox. The oiler did just what it sounds like, he oiled. He kept all the cups and cavities filled with oils and mixed the different oils, kept the oil cans filled and generally took care of all the rotating machinery, not just the main engines. He was also the engineer's right hand man and handled the controls when the engineer needed a break and also helped adjust and tighten the constantly loosening large nuts and bolts on the vibrating machinery with large wrenches and a small sledge hammer. The wiper was just under the oiler in the pecking order and with large brushes he would "wipe" the rotating and parts of the reciprocating engine which were exposed with a grease and/or heavy oil. He was also the clean-up man and wiped the constantly running oil off the engines and decks where it would get thrown. They all had to work together and it was constant chores in the engine rooms of steam boats but they divvied the work. 24 hour boats had a gang for each watch but a lot of the ones I remembered were day boats and only had one crew on at a time. Later, when the big old direct drive diesels were popular there was one engineer and one oiler to a watch. The boats were still bell boats and while the engineer operated the engine the oiler kept everything running and lubricated. Still later with more modern oiling systems and bigger and better air compressors they cut down to one oiler on board at a time. When the "modern" 2 cycle engines came into use during and just after WW II and had pilothouse control, the engineers could do most of the maintenance because they weren't operating the engine manually and they cut back to an oiler only on the chief's watch. So for a week, two weeks or 10 days depending on the schedule there was no oiler on the boat. Then came automation and they did away with the oilers altogether. And as soon as they were sure the automation worked and the union approved, they cut back to one engineer on the boat at a time.

    I went a couple of more times with my father but during the late 1940's, through the 1950's and early 1960's McAllister was converting steamboats to diesel one after another. U.S. Navy LST's (Landing Ship Tank) from WW II were being scrapped by the government and the power plants, running gear and auxiliary equipment were being bought up by tug companies at bargain prices. My father was one of the few along with A.J. McAllister Sr. and Red Edmunds, the McAllister Port Engineer who were allowed to go into Witte's yard on Staten Island and pick out what they wanted and get along with John Witte. If John Witte didn't like you he didn't sell to you. In fact, he told you to get out of his yard! Eddy Todd, McAllister President and ex Steam engineer was one of the people who used to go to Witte's and also to government surplus places in Baltimore and buy surplus machinery in bulk. My father had worked for Bethlehem Steel in Staten Island during the war as an Outside Machinist Foreman. One of his main jobs was to align the engines, reduction gears and tail shafts in Destroyer Escorts that they were building there. He got to work closely with the representative from the Falk Gear Company. (Later on I worked with the same man in Tug & Barge Dry Docks shipyard) So each time they were ready to do an alignment of the propulsion machinery on a tug they had converted at McAllister's Black Tom yard in Caven Point, Bayonne, they would bring my father in for the couple or three days it took to get it done. After awhile they were doing so many they just brought him in permanent as the outside machinist foreman.

Robert Mattsson

## Chapter 2 - Black Tom Yard

During the early 1950's when I was thirteen and my brother Mel was twelve we would go with my father on Saturdays to Black Tom when he was working as often as he would let us. That's where we learned to drive in his old stick shift Studebaker. He also let us drive the yard truck and a small three wheeled crane. After a few times he trusted us in the yard and pretty much gave us free reign. We would play captain in the five or six wooden pilothouses that were on the docks waiting to be stripped and scrapped. Mel and I would play on the barge that had the machine shop, carpenters shop and locker room on it and we had the use of a small row boat that we would use to catch crabs and swim from. Caven Point yard had a unique bathroom. A three sided shed on the pier that had a wooden plank settee with holes in that went right into the water. My brother and I thought this was really neat and we couldn't wait to take a dump and watch it go down. Especially at low tide. What a splash! Right after that we would go swimming and crabbing in the same water.

This picture of the Black Tom yard has been posted on tugboats@yahoo.com many times and I can't find who to credit. We would also roam around on all the tugs and wooden barges. We would go crabbing along the pilings standing on the 40 foot long by 3 foot diameter logs used for fendering. The logs were slippery and we fell off many times holding onto the dock piles and then climbing back on the fenders. By the end of the day we were covered with tar, grease, green stuff and who knows what. My father would stand us on the pier, wipe us down with diesel oil and wash us off with a fire hose. Boy, that hurt and a couple of times he almost knocked us off the pier. The next time we went through the same routine though so I guess it wasn't all that bad.

## Chapter 3 - Tug & Barge Yard

In 1955 McAllister took over the Jersey Central Railroad Marine Repair Yard at Dock 19 Jersey City, New Jersey and moved north. Part of the deal was to continue the repair of the railroad's ferries, barges and tugs belonging to Jersey Central. Included in the yard was something McAllister needed sorely and that was dry docks. There were three, Dock 1 was of 2000 ton capacity when she was new but was now getting old and the hole under her was filling in so she couldn't go down too deep. She could however, still raise the ferries that although they were not too heavy, they were wide with their deck sponsons coming out on both sides and so needed the full width of that dock. Dock 2 was 1200 ton capacity and still capable of lifting most of McAllister's and the railroads tugs. She also lifted the car floats easily. Dock three was the newest and had a capacity of 1000 tons. This dock was strong and could lift the big tugs near the apron ends without hogging as long as the dock master knew what he was doing.

From sixteen to eighteen I was in and out of school and in and out of trouble. I couldn't wait to turn eighteen. Eighteen meant I could drive legally, drink in bars and clubs legally and get to work in the shipyard. I started at Tug & Barge Dry Docks Inc. on my eighteenth birthday,

November 6, 1957. What joy, all of the above and the promise of a pay check to boot! My father drove as I didn't have my license yet and we picked up the two car pool members in Staten Island, then over the Bayonne Bridge to Avenue E, a stop at Slim's Bar, then to Garfield Avenue, right on to Chapel Road, over the tracks (cursing if we had to wait for a train) left on Caven Point Road, a quick right and then left onto Burma Road and then a right onto the unpaved road to the yard.

The last part of the trip to Dock 19 took us through marshland with high swamp grass on either side of a very bumpy cinder road with fluorescent yellow spots and roaming wild dogs. Some of the holes in the road you actually drove into and out of, they were so big. And the bottom of the car would scrape along the chassis. The cinders came from the powerhouse owned by Jersey Central that was adjacent to the shipyard and made the electricity, compressed air and steam for the yard itself and the coal dumping operation on dock 18. The yellow fluorescent stuff was chromium residue dumped along the road from a bleach plant nearby. The dogs were not a problem during the day but turned vicious at night. What was really neat though was as you got close to the yard and the water you would look straight down the road heading southeast and see the back of the Statue of Liberty. Even from the back it was beautiful and we never got tired of looking at her. Later on in life when I was a Port engineer I would be called in for breakdowns at 2 or 3 o'clock in the morning and get to see the Statue all lit up at night, still beautiful. Once in the yard you could also see Ellis Island beyond the coal dumpers on Dock 18, Governors Island across the bay and the buildings jutting up on Manhattan Island. The harbor was always busy with tugs, barges, lighters, ships, ferries and pleasure craft. It was amazing to me and I was told repeatedly during my first year to stop gazing at all of this and get back to work.

The yard had seven permanent brick buildings, the general storeroom with the main office above it, the lumber mill, the carpenters shop, the machine shop, the locker room combined with the diesel parts storeroom, the blacksmith or plate shop and the fender loft. There were many other smaller offices and storage sheds scattered around the yard. Most of these were old barge cabins, pilothouses and some steel sheds fabricated by the yard. Everything was heated by the steam from the next door power plant through underground and overhead pipe lines. Steam could be seen condensing from the air vents, water traps and just plain leaks. This gave the place a special kind of atmosphere. My father dropped me off near the locker room, told me to go find a locker and be in the machine shop ready for work at 7:20, along with the outside machinists, the gang I would be based in. He didn't take me in and assign me a locker, I guess because he didn't want to embarrass me or himself. The guys were great though and showed me to a locker. Even this was exciting to me. After changing we all made our way en mass to the yard proper. Me and others to the machine shop, the rest to their assigned places. My father came in at 7:20 on the nose and told us what we would be doing today and who we would be working with. I don't think anybody really wanted to work with this skinny kid who was the boss's son but I was assigned and the day was about to begin. At 7:30 the whistle blew to start the day and you could hear machinery starting in the machine shop and the men from the other gangs walking out to their jobs. As a helper I got to carry the mechanics tool box and any of the larger tools he needed that we checked out of the tool room. Once we were settled in the engine room of a tug that was being overhauled, the mechanic I was working under, Walter, the Baron, Baronoski made a show of asking me to go to the storeroom. I was to get a 5 pound bucket of steam with a number two cover. This made sense because it was cold down there. One of the other mechanics, Jerry Nardi, who was rigging a chain fall, told me to get him two 5/8" sky hooks while I was there and to charge them to this tug. The five pounds of steam I could remember but the 5/8" sky hooks I wrote in the little spiral pad my father told me to carry. Being early, the storeroom was crowded and as I didn't know the protocol I just kind of hung back waiting for my turn. I guess they knew something was up though and the guys let me go ahead of them. When the storekeeper finished with the fellow in front of me, he gruffly asked what I wanted. When I told him, the whole place cracked up and he pulled out a two foot piece of rubber hose, slammed it down on the sheet metal lined counter with a crack and came running around the counter as though he was going to kill me with that hose. I took off from there like a bat out of hell and realized how stupid I was. I was embarrassed and kind of lost my big shot attitude. I went back to the tug and told them they were all out of what they wanted and the storekeeper would order it for them. The next big event was the coffee truck, the 'roach coach' that usually came around 9:30 when the break whistle was blown. Fifteen minutes of coffee, donut or sandwich, cigarettes and sitting around talking about every topic imaginable. I was with the big people and I loved it. Sports, bosses, politics, women and jobs were discussed with a lot of cursing thrown in.

That reminds me, when we were driving home that evening my father was complaining about one of the foremen and what he had done that day. Well, he was cursing up a storm. I had never heard him curse before except for a couple of mild ones in the house. I was really worried what my mother would say if he kept this up. Talking and cursing all the way home and driving up our street and me not saying anything, probably my jaw was hanging. When the front tires of his Chevy station wagon that he had at the time hit the driveway he kept on as fervently as before but with no cursing at all. He continued the story without cursing all the way into the house until he kissed my mother hello. I learned something about my father that day. Even when he cursed though it didn't sound all that bad as he still had his Norwegian accent even though he had been in the United States since he was 18 years old.

That reminds me of the time he came home and announced he was going to buy one of those new little cars from Germany, a WolksVagon. My sister Maureen laughed so hard I thought she was going to choke. Any time any of her friends came over she asked my father to tell them what kind of car he was going to buy. He did and they all laughed. I know if me or one of my brothers did this we would get cracked in the back of the head but she got away with it. Not without a sense of humor, he came home one evening and told us he changed his mind. He was not going to buy a WolksVagon but decided he would buy a Wolwo. Well, we all cracked up including my father.

# Chapter 4 - Typical Day

So a typical morning went like this…

"Good morning Pop" I said to my father, Arne. "Good morning Robert, get your coffee we have to go." "Okay Pop but I'm going to have some cereal too" I said. He just nodded. My father was reading yesterday's afternoon paper, the Staten Island Advance, eating toast and putting sugar from the sugar bowl into his mouth and then sipping his coffee. This drove my mother crazy but she wasn't up to see him. He would dip his spoon in his coffee and say that it cleaned the spoon but I think it was just to get more sugar to stick to the spoon. Oh well… another normal day. It was a nice morning, late spring, sunny and getting warm already. Just as I was finishing my breakfast he folded the paper, got up and put the dishes in the sink in almost one motion. He didn't look at the clock but instinctively knew it was time to go. I looked; it was 6:20, the time we always left. I put my stuff away while he grabbed the lunches my mother had made the night before from the Frigidaire. He also took another small bag from inside. It was a real GM Frigidaire with two ice cube trays and enough room for two frozen packages of vegetables and one can of frozen orange juice. That was it. Out into the backyard we went, closing the backdoor to the kitchen hall but not locking it. We never locked it unless we were going away for a couple of days and that was rare. There was only one key anyway and it was always hanging up behind one of the coats that hung from the hooks on the back hall wall.

It was a beautiful day, you could smell the grass and dew from the yard. We got in my father's 1951 Chevrolet station wagon that was parked in the two ribbon driveway. It was forest green with faux wood trim and had six cylinders and a standard three speed manual shift. Not my idea of a cool car but it was fun to drive. It was my father's week to drive so we picked up two guys that worked with us at the shipyard, Claude the iron worker and Little Richie, the telephone operator. Tug & Barge Dry Docks was located behind the Statue of Liberty in Jersey City at Exit 14 B on the NJ Turnpike. We didn't take the turnpike for the one exit from Bayonne though, unless we were late because it cost 10 cents.
Once we picked everyone up, we headed for the Staten Island side of the Bayonne Bridge and paid the toll with our 30 day discount ticket book that we passed from car to car each week. At that time you had to stop and pay each way and my father and his cronies were friendly with the toll takers who were the same people almost all the time. You weren't allowed to use the ticket book from car to car but the toll people never said anything. It was tough for everyone at the time, that's why we car pooled.

Once we were over the bridge we made our way East and North to Avenue E and Slim's Bar & Grill. Everybody got out including me; sometimes I just stayed in the car and read the newspaper that one of the guys, Claude, brought with him each morning. But today I wanted to get some of Slim's clam juice that was set up at the end of the bar. This area wasn't too crowded but the rest of the bar area was four and five deep. The standard breakfast here was a shot of whisky and a beer, usually twice for each man. No time was wasted; Slim knew everyone and what they wanted. He set it up on the bar, it was passed back and the money passed forward without anyone speaking. The clam juice was free. This was typical of the many bars in Bayonne.
Thirst wetted, we got back in the Chevy and made our way through the back roads of Bayonne and Jersey City to the long and bumpy dirt road through the marsh that led to the shipyard. We were met by the 16 or so barking dogs that populated the yard and parked the station wagon up against an old piling encrusted with barnacles. My father opened the bag he brought and threw the bones and fat he brought from home to

the dogs. He then went to his office which was a really neat old wooden barge cabin. I thought it was great and would make a wonderful hut in the woods. Claude and I made our way to the old Central Railroad of New Jersey locker room with the big, round common ceramic sinks with multiple water outlets (all cold), skinny dark green lockers, broken windows and pigeon shit. The din from a hundred and fifty or so guys getting ready to go to work was loud but not overbearing and comforting in a way. "Hello to you, hi to you, mornin', hey, how are ya. What you got for lunch? Anybody got good hot peppers? Who's your foreman today? Gotta hangover? What numbers did you play? What have you got on the hip? Watchca think, will we work Saturday? Hey kid, your father giving you a soft job today? Where did you leave off yesterday? I hear there is a lay-off coming. No, no, I hear we have a conversion coming up from Philly. I hate that Labor Foreman. You hate every Foreman. You gotta buck? I owe the coffee man." Typical morning small talk as we took off our street clothes and put on our diesel fuel and smoke smelling work clothes full of asbestos and sandblast dust. We grabbed our hard hats and went to our separate areas to get our morning orders from our respective foremen. The inside machinists met in front of the machine shop tool room, the outside machinists or mechanics met in the machine shop in front of the mechanics heavy tool room, the carpenters and dockhands met by the saw mill, the iron workers inside the plate shop, the laborers outside the labor foreman's office, the electricians just inside the machine shop main door and the crane operator and riggers just went to their equipment and started them to get them warmed up and ready so when they were asked to make a lift they were prepared.

Robert Mattsson

# Chapter 5 - Cranes

The big job in the yard when I started was the conversion of the Margaret M. McAllister from steam to diesel. When I started most of the main machinery and boiler had already been removed but now we were removing piping and valves to be cleaned and recycled, and getting the hull ready for the engine and reduction gear bed frame and the installation of a new fuel tank. This was the main job but almost every day some of us were pulled off to work on a breakdown on a working tug that needed some minor repair or a fender re-hung. That reminds of the time we had to make a repair on the steam whistle on the tug Du Bois II. I was the helper to Gomez, the second in charge pipe fitter. We had to go up to the top of the stack on the Dubois and repair a pipe leak to the steam whistle. You couldn't work off a ladder so we were lifted in a bucket or three sided utility box with our tools to make the repair. You can see how high in the picture of from the *Dan Owen Collection*. My father was making the lift as the crane operator was busy elsewhere. My father

Steam tug Dubois II

could operate all the cranes in the yard including the old wooden hulled stick lighter. He taught me to operate all the cranes also and I became proficient at all of them except this stick lighter. There were too many levers and foot pedals for one guy as far as I was concerned. Anyway, this day he was operating one of the three rail cranes we had. He lifted us up to the top of the Du Bois stack with our tools and we made the repair. We had to yell to someone to get him back because he went off to do something else while we were up there working. When he finally came back, he swung us over the water between the Du Bois and the dock and began lowering us into the water. Gomez was screaming, my father was laughing and I, who always had his gloves on as I was taught when working with steam, grabbed the cable of the hook fall that was on the way up instead of the one coming down. Gomez went in the water up to his thighs and my father began yelling for me to let go of the cable because I was on the way up. The rest of the yard came to look and laugh. Gomez was in the water screaming in Spanish, me hanging like a monkey on the cable and my father outside the crane cab yelling at me to let go so he could lift the bucket again without me getting my hands caught in the sheaves. Anyway it worked out and I got a little more respect after that. So... back to the Margaret.

  We were removing valves as I said and one day after filling a bucket with valves we were removing from the engine room to the after deck we needed a crane operator to take them to the storeroom. The main guy, Sam, was busy so I got the job. Great! Now was the time to show off. I had come in many a Saturday on my own time to get proficient on the cranes and now was the time to show my stuff. I lifted the bucket as neat as could be, brought the boom around so it was perpendicular with the tracks and took off backwards with the load towards the storeroom. Now, my plan was to fly down the track at full speed, swing the boom and load, counter clockwise as I approached the storeroom and then flip on the air brake so I would be able to lower the load in front of the storeroom door, all in one smooth motion. So as I was traveling, I swung the boom and crane house left while I started to lower the load and flipped the air break. The air line for the brakes came up through the center pin of the crane turntable and as the crane turned and turned over the years it had been wearing. Well, the air line picked this moment to break in a blast of compressed air and I had no brakes. Now the crane and the load are headed for the storeroom so all I could do was jerk the boom back to the right. This snapped the load like a whip and it swung up and hit the building at the juncture between the storeroom and the second floor of the main office where the Superintendent's office was. The place was raining brass valves, people were running for their life and the Superintendent, Joe Weber, came out on the balcony of the back stairway and started to scream at me, calling me all kinds of shipyard names. I was no longer the hotshot crane operator I thought I was but it did teach me to take it easier. And of course I was ribbed about it for weeks, because there is nothing better than making fun of the boss's son! The regular crane operator, Sam, was seen with a big smile on his face also. My father made me make the repair to the brake lines and this was my first experience with a rotary air valve so it was a good learning experience. Sam had his own problem not two weeks later when he was lifting one of the yard utility buckets off a wooden barge. The bucket was about 5 feet wide, 8 feet long and on three sides about 3 feet high, and one end being open. The barge had been used for a load of coal and the leavings were shoveled up and put into the bucket. This made it very heavy and when he lifted it and had it at the right height to swing the boom he set the boom cable drum ratchet but the crane being old and the load heavy it distorted the thick deck of the crane house where the ratchet was locked. When he released the boom clutch the ratchet sprung free and the load came down so fast he couldn't do anything about it. He almost killed the rigger who always walked under the load no matter how many times you yelled at him. Well, the rigger heard the sound of the cable screaming as it unwound on the drum and jumped out of the way just as the bucket landed and went right through the wooden deck of the barge with only a third of it showing at a 45 degree angle. There was a big to do but only because of the labor it would take to rig it free and repair the barge. The crane was never examined or repaired even though Sam told them how it happened. They thought he just screwed up.

Some time went by and I had to take this same crane out to our dump that was about a quarter mile away in the swamp. We dumped all our garbage, sawdust, shavings, rags and old pilings and wood from barge and tug repairs here and burned it. The pile never really went out even in most heavy rains, it just kept smoldering. If it did go out we brought down a gallon of diesel oil, poured it on the pile and relit it. This day we had a load of garbage and when we reached the site I swung the yard bucket out, lowered the bucket and the rigger released the two slings that were on the open end and I raised the bucket to empty it. That accomplished, I swung it around and down so the rigger could reattach the two front slings. I raised the bucket as high as I could without 2 blocking it so that I could see under it and so it wouldn't swing around so much as the track was uneven and bumpy. The rigger took his usual spot on a platform on the right front of the crane and I engaged the drive wheels and put the throttle to full speed, which was all of about 10 miles per hour. We were rolling along fine through the tall swamp reeds and I was standing at the controls feeling pretty good with a nice breeze coming into the crane house but the crane was surging right and left because of the crooked track and the speed of the crane. I didn't think much of it, but all of a sudden the boom ratchet came free because of all the twisting. The boom cables went straight up at my right and left arms and when they started to fly by me I pulled in my arms instinctively and just gawked as the boom came down with a bang on top of the bucket and the crushed bucket was screeching along the tracks with sparks flying until I came to my senses and pulled back the throttle and set the brakes. I called out for the rigger and when I didn't get an answer I was sure I killed him. When I jumped down off the crane I saw him crawling out of the swamp about 100 yards back. He had jumped for his life when he saw the boom coming down. Later on my father told me I was lucky that the bucket landed square on the tracks because if the boom had landed in the rail ties it would have dug in, sheared the hinge pins that were right in front of the operator and it would have come straight back and cut me in half. The crane was repaired after that and Sam was vindicated even though no one acknowledged it.

Another time Sam was on the 20 ton Grove, a four wheel tired crane and was traveling with a tail shaft slung from the hook. Traveling with a load on a tired crane is a no no, but was done regularly at the yard. Whenever you lift anything of any weight you are supposed to have your outriggers extended. Well, the roadway in and about the yard was not paved and there were big bumps and dips in it. One of the painters had been hurt on the job and while he was out on disability he bought a fairly new, but used, bright yellow Chevrolet station wagon and brought it into the yard to show us. Because he didn't plan on staying and he wanted all of us to see the car, he didn't park in the lot but brought it up to the office and parked in a no parking area. Along came Sam in the crane with the tail shaft swinging back and forth and the rigger trying to hold onto the tag line. Just as he got abreast of Bill's car a dip caused the load to swing violently to

his right and pulled the crane right over on its side. Unfortunately for Bill that's where his car was. The crane boom flattened the car and totaled it. I remember looking at it and the tires all appeared to be blown out. But when we lifted the Grove off the car, all the tires came back to shape! The company didn't want to pay him for the car because he was in a no parking zone but after a period of time he was eventually reimbursed.

There were advantages and disadvantages to being the boss's son. Among the disadvantages were being ribbed all the time because I was one of the boss's sons. I had to work hard to prove I was my own man and I got all the hard and dirty jobs because my father didn't want anyone to think I was getting preferential treatment. Among the advantages though, I learned to work hard, I learned a lot by having to do these hard and dirty jobs and the fact that my father, who wanted to make sure I knew the business, put me with every gang and with every foreman. He also let me come in on Saturdays and use any equipment, crane or machinery I wanted to. Saturday usually had a much smaller contingent of people working because it was time and a half and they were usually the better and the senior people. It was also a slower pace on Saturday. When they saw that I was trying to learn something on my own time they would show me the right way and help to get me material to work with. I had the best of the best teaching me to use a lathe, different ways of using an Oxy-Acetylene torch and the right and wrong way to weld. And why DC current was different than AC current to name a few. I even learned how to caulk and how to use a large, wood planer. I would also practice on all the cranes including the electric overhead crane in the machine shop. The machine shop foreman, Adam Guthry, was very particular about who operated the crane. Landing a tail shaft in a lathe is a very delicate operation, as is lifting a large ball bearing out of very hot oil and holding it in position so the machinists can fit it over a reduction gear shaft. I eventually earned his trust, but it took a long time.

During the repowering of the Margaret, the pipe fitter Gomez was piping up a 2" fuel fill line at the top of the new fuel tank and called me over to pull down on a 4 x 4 to bend the pipe down and make up a pipe union because they didn't line up. I did as told and he managed to get it together. I didn't think much of it at the time as I had watched him and Eddie Shultz do this before. After forcing a pipe, they would come back and heat it with an oxy-acetylene torch so it would soften, bend somewhat and take the pressure off. Some years later when I was the oiler on the Margaret, I had to go on top of the tank and disconnect this same union. There was about 2' of clearance between the top of the fuel tank and the deck above it. I was having a real hard time unscrewing it as it was real tight and not much room for me and the pipe wrench. I was leaning over the pipe to get a good purchase with my neck just above the pipe. At the last second I remembered how we made it fit and pulled my head back just as the union came free and the pipe sprung up with such force it hit the deck above it with a loud bang and dented the steel plate. If I hadn't pulled my head back just at the right time it would probably have broke my neck. I guess they forgot to heat that pipe up!

Robert Mattsson

# Chapter - 6 Labor Gang

The gang I least wanted to work in was the labor gang. Even though some of the jobs were interesting, the foreman, Stoney, was a hard man to work for. Once in awhile when the Jersey Central Rail Road ferries were in for an overhaul, and I wasn't needed as a helper in the engine room. I would have to work for Stony in the labor gang and one of the jobs was to clean off the wooden passenger benches with Oakite, a very caustic cleaner we used to get them ready for re-varnishing. We had to wear rubber gloves to prevent the solution from eating into our skin. On one of these occasions the gloves I was given had holes in them. Worse, they were small holes, so the gloves filled up with the solution but would not drain back out again. After a while my hands started to burn so I took the gloves off. When Stony snuck up on us, as he always did, he gave me hell for not having my gloves on. I explained that the gloves have holes in them, but he said, we have no more and I have to wear them or go home. I put them on and by lunchtime the skin of my hands had cracked and they were bleeding.

At lunch break I went to my father and told him the situation. He said, what did Stony say? I told him and he said "if I couldn't do it, I would have to go home". So my father said, "Well I guess you'll have to go home then". How am I going to get home I asked, I drove in with you? That's up to you he said. So I changed my clothes, but it was hard for me to do, as blood was getting all over my Levi's. After getting dressed I was able to catch the yard truck going on a parts run. He dropped me off on Garfield Avenue in Jersey City, where I waited for the local bus. When the bus finally came I couldn't get my hands in my pocket to pay the driver because the skin of my hands had shrunk and pulled them into tight fists. I got no sympathy from the driver however, who went into my pockets to get the money. The bus only ran to the Bayonne Bridge, but not over it to Staten Island. I hitchhiked over the bridge, but it was hard to stick out my thumb. I finally got a ride and he let me off at Forest Avenue on Staten Island. Two more buses and a half mile walk and I got home 15 minutes before my father. I told my mother what happened and she was fuming and waited for my father at the door to give him hell. He wasn't very happy, but I was smirking. After applying hand lotion all night the skin on my hands loosened up enough for me to go back to work the next day.

    Another time Stony sent me into a compartment of a car float that was on dry dock to paint it out with red lead paint using a roller. Well, when you are in a compartment of a barge on dry dock in the summer rolling paint, any paint, it gets real hot and fumy. I was in the compartment alone and without a blower and starting to get dizzy. At coffee break I went to my father who told me (yep, you guessed it) to go to Stony. I went to Stony and he said there were no more blowers available, but I could go to the Superintendent, Joe Weber and complain to him. I don't think he thought I would do it but I did. Joe Weber didn't appear too happy with me either, but I think he knew what was right. He brought me to the iron workers tool room and picked the heaviest electric blower he could find and told me to carry it up to the car float on dry dock and set it up. It was electric, so I had to go to the electrical foreman, Steve and beg for some heavy extension cords, believe it or not they were hard to come by in the yard. Anyway, he got me a couple and after I lugged everything up to the dry dock and then up a ladder to the deck of the car float and down into the compartment and connected everything, I finally got it working. I was a happy but tired painter. At lunch I was needled endlessly about what a baby and troublemaker I was, as the story had spread all over the yard. Later, some of the guys, especially from the labor gang came up to me and said "Good going, we need someone to speak up once in a while".

# Chapter - 7 Electricians Gang

One gang I really liked to work with was the electricians. Steve Zachery was the foreman and he was a real quiet, meticulous and smart man. He taught me a whole lot. I learned a lot about electricity but I also learned that being an electrician was being able to do a lot of mechanical work. We ran steel flat bar runways for the cables, drilled and tapped the holes for the screws to hold the cable clamps, I broke many taps and drills before I got the knack. However, I learned how to remove broken taps and drills after all my mistakes. We even made the cable clamps ourselves. Then you had to pull the cables and attach them to the runways. All the cables at that time were marine, lead armored cable that was heavy and pretty hard to bend. At each bulkhead we had to pass the cable through watertight glands. When the cable reached its destination we had to cut back the mesh armor, cut through the lead sheathing (without cutting into the cable) and then strip the cable proper. If you made a mistake and cut through the cable you had to pray there was enough slack to pull it up six inches and do it again the right way. Steve would show me where the connections were to be wired to in the starting box, motor or switchboard, but again this was more or less mechanical stuff done with a screwdriver or wrench. That reminds of the time I was adding an inch and a quarter by a quarter inch thick copper buss bar behind a D.C. switchboard on a tug. The switchboard was live (as they usually were) and I had to drill holes in the existing buss bar and attach a new one. Everything went fine until the very end as I was tightening the quarter inch cap screws and my 7/16" socket wrench hit the opposite polarity buss bar just above it. There was a crack and a blinding flash, I instinctively jumped back and hit my head on a hull frame. I thought I was dead. When I came to my senses and got my sight back, I saw that my wrench had one end melted off and my hand was burned. Steve came over and told me to be more careful and went back to work as if nothing had happened. No one cared about my hand, but I was very careful after that.

Steve would show me how things were wired and more importantly, why. He showed me how starting boxes worked, how to change the fusible links in large fuses, how carbon piles worked, how reverse current relays worked, how to properly connect wires in a junction box and many more things without ever holding anything back. Steve was very vain about his hair or lack of it though. A few of the workers my age told me we had to peek into his office/shack when he changed clothes at the end of the day. I didn't want to pry but my curiosity got the better of me. So we snuck up and peeked into the window of his shack. He would wash up, and change his clothes while keeping his hard hat on. At the last minute he would reach up for his fedora and quickly swap that for his hard hat. You hardly had time to see his head as he did it in a flash. He was totally bald.

# Chapter - 8 Trying to Break In

When I started in the tug business (right about the time dinosaurs became extinct) it was very difficult if not impossible to get a job on the tugs. First there was the Catch 22 situation, no job unless you had a union card, no union card unless you had a job. Even family members had a tough time getting in. But if you were adamant and persevered there was always a crack you could squeeze through. Many good captains and docking pilots started by 'hamming', guys who would go out on a tug with a family member or friend of the family and work for the week or two on board for nothing but their meals and whatever skills they could glean from the deckhand and mate. You had to hope the deckhand was willing to teach you and also what he taught, was the right thing. And you got to do all of the deckhand's rotten jobs, like cleaning the heads, mopping the companionways, washing the pilot house windows and bringing the captain his coffee. And paint, paint, paint! But in return you were taught how to splice, how to throw a line (and not call it a rope), how to flip it off a bitt and how to anticipate what the captains next move would be. All valuable information if you planned to stay in the business. They even let you steer and land a light tug once in awhile. Most deckhands and crews could figure out real quick if you were cut out for tug boating and would either shun you if you didn't work hard or seemed uninterested, or hold you close, rib you and give you the inside scoop if you were serious and gave it your all. This went for everyone, whether you were an obscure relative of the oiler or your last name was McAllister (and there were plenty of McAllister's going through and they all worked hard). All this work and time put in and there was no guarantee of getting hired. Some guys 'hammed' for more than 6 months before they got a job. No one was treated special either, as I found out during my oiler days. My father Arne was the outside machinist foreman and assistant superintendent of Tug & Barge Dry Docks where I got my start. I did every dirty job there was in the yard but always was taken to task for standing on the bulkhead or pier watching the tugs maneuver because that is where I really longed to be. My main job was outside machinist helper and then finally outside machinist first class. I was also a crane operator, laborer, electrician, carpenters helper, iron workers helper, deckhand on the yard workboat and

storekeeper, but my heart wasn't in it, I longed to be on the tugs. I decked the workboat M.L. Edwards around '58 or '59. Our main jobs were to deliver line, coal and kerosene to the deck barges, covered barges and stick lighters that McAllister owned including Lee &

Simmons and Manhattan Lighterage. We also collected all the old worn out line from the barges to bring back to the yard to make fenders. In the yard itself besides shifting we would hang and fasten the rope fenders on the tugs and make some small lifts and bring propellers out to the dry dock ends for the tugs we were changing the propellers on. We also stored the excess junk line in our hold and when we got enough we would go over to Brooklyn, under the Brooklyn Bridge on the East side, sell it and split the money. Boy, what a bonus! I felt I was rich. I searched real hard for scrap line after that.

If I remember correctly the M.L. Edwards was scrapped at Dock 19. I remember being told she was a real busy little lighter during WW II running ammo for the government. When I was on it she had a Grey Marine 6-71 for power and a GM 2-71 for the winches and boom. Early in the morning, even before the whistle, I would get her coal stove in the hold going to get a little heat. Then I started the General Motors 2-71 hoisting engine to warm it up and the biggest thrill of all was loading the Grey Marine 6-71 main engine up with ether from a plastic bulb put in its holder, puncturing it, pumping in into the engine, lighting a fuel soaked rag on the end of a piece of 3/8" round bar and holding it over the intake of the blower while you cranked and prayed that it would start. It took a relatively long time cranking over while sucking in the flame from the fuel soaked rag, but it always did start.

# Chapter - 9 Alignment

Alignment - The J.P. McAllister was put on Dock 3, way back with the stern over the dry dock apron to facilitate rudder removal. This was a particularly tough job for the dock master because all the weight was concentrated over the last two compartments of the dock and put a lot of strain on the bulkheads. The dock master had to keep flooding the forward compartments to keep the dock even. We only had about 4 or 5 inches freeboard on the dock. The rudder was dropped through the apron opening and the wheel and tail shaft changed out at this time. After reinstalling the tail shaft coupling and checking the alignment, my father said we could not connect the tail shaft coupling because the alignment would change when we got in the water. He told us that not only was the dry dock bending but the tug also. To make his point he ran a wire from the top of the stack to the stern rail and attached a strain gauge. When the tug came off dock his plan was to show me how much the hull had distorted while on the blocks. Well, as we went into the water and even before we were fully afloat, the gauge went to its maximum and the wire broke. Point taken, lesson learned. Another time I wanted to finish up an alignment on a tug and my father told me I would have to wait until morning because we had a very sunny and warm day. I said, "So?". He told me to take my readings, write them down and check them again in the morning and I would see the difference. He was right of course, the sun shining on the portside for most of the day twisted the hull just enough to change the readings by .015". Another lesson learned.

Another time I was aligning the tail and intermediate shafts on a Jersey Central ferry and we were using oak blocks for the main shims under the intermediate bearings and then shim stock. I figured the closer I could get the oak block to fit, the better and the less cutting of shim stock I would have to do. So I took the readings and went to

George Pillepich, the carpenter Foreman and told him to take .018" off one side and taper it down to .023" on the other side. He went crazy and started yelling at me and at the same time pulling me towards my father's office. He wanted to know if I thought he was running a machine shop or a carpenter's shop, that the closest he could do for me was a 16th of an inch and that was pushing it, an 8th of an inch was more like it. He was still yelling when we got to my father's office. My father listened and told George he would take care of it. He sat me down and explained that I was trying to be too exact, that there was room to be off a little on a long run of shafting like that on the ferries. He said that I would be amazed if I saw some alignments and also how after six months or so, everything changed. With that, he said lets go for a ride. We went up to the Jersey Central ferry terminal in Jersey City and got on the next ferry to Manhattan. Down into the engine room we went, said hello to the crew who all knew my father and into the shaft alley. Well, it was amazing, the shafts were wobbling and oscillating and the line shaft bearings as well. My father said the ferry came out of the yard six months ago and will be back in six months from now but they will keep running this way because they have lived with it before and it hasn't been a problem. We usually aligned engines and reduction gears and set them on steel shims that were machined to very close tolerances and then used tin or brass shim stock to get it exact. At one time we tried to use phenolic (Mycarta) blocks. We did this on more than one engine and found out shortly that when they got oil soaked, they expanded enough to throw off the alignment and we had to bring the boats in and redo the alignment. That's about the time we started to use Chock Fast, a two part plastic/epoxy type of liquid that we mixed and poured into place. We would build dams of light flat bar and special foam to hold the liquid in place. When it set up about an hour later it was as hard as a rock and didn't shrink or expand.

# Chapter 10 My Big Break

I begged my father and the port engineer at the time, Red Edmunds, for an oiler's job on the tugs but to no avail. Then came the crack I was waiting for, an oiler on the Theresa McAllister, a wooden hulled, direct drive diesel called in sick and there was no one available to replace him that afternoon and the crew would not operate the tug without an oiler. I was pressed into service because I was at the right place at the right time. That only lasted a week but at least I was an unofficial oiler. So as relief jobs came up I got them and one day while hanging on at the Port Richmond,

Staten Island water dock, the union delegate, Al Conetti came on board the Margaret McAllister where I was filling in, asked me for my union card and when he found out I didn't have one, he forced me to join and sent Larry Nielson a union delegate down to the tug to collect my money. Boy was I happy, now I was an official oiler and had seniority, the lowest, but still, union seniority. It cost me $250 initiation fee but I was able to pay it off in installments so it wasn't so bad. That was a lot of money at the time.

Speaking of the Theresa, she was a bell boat and had a direct reversible engine and a wooden hull. The Teresa was a relatively small boat but was used for everything from moving scows to helping on ship dockings, as were all McAllister boats. She was being used as a day boat at the time and the oiler went off sick. They needed someone in a hurry and took me from the shipyard as they needed someone right away and no one else was available on such short notice. Naturally, I was very, very excited and happy to get on board. I was brought out to her by one of McAllister's steam tugs with whatever clothes and gear I could pull from my locker. The chief was a young fellow, and he had been up quite a while, but he took me below and showed me the lower engine room and how to operate the main engine, and also how to understand the bells as it was a bell boat that was operated by the engineer from the lower engine room. He stayed with me for a while and taught me the bell system, but he was tired and needed a nap. He told me if I didn't understand the bells to wait, and I would get the signal again as the Captain would understand if I didn't answer and he would repeat the bells. The engine room was really neat, I had been in it a few times before when she came to the yard for repairs but never as a crew member. Besides a shaft driven DC generator she had a single cylinder 71 series General Motors engine driving an 8 KW generator and a 2-71 GM of 20 KW. Typical of a wooden boat she leaked constantly and there was a bilge pump built onto the main engine and it ran the whole time the engine was running. There was of course an electric pump also if the engine pump couldn't keep up or the boat was lying idle. When the engine was running the lights were fairly bright but in the stop or dead slow mode, the shaft generator didn't turn fast enough to make enough voltage and the electrical system went to batteries that were near the end of their life and the lights dimmed and any electric motors that were running would slow down. The main air compressor was run off the tail shaft with large vee belts like the generator, so as long as we kept running and didn't do a lot of shifting, we had enough compressed air to start and restart the main engine without using the electric motor driven air compressor. We were doing some scow shifting in the East River when I was put onboard and when finished we headed down the Kills to Elizabeth Port, New Jersey, known to all as E Port. Enroute, the engineer went to lie down and reminded me about not understanding a signal, that I should wait for more bells if I didn't understand (you can see where this is going, right?). The trip was really uneventful, I had a couple of single gongs to slow down to half and then a jingle to hook it up again and once I even got two gongs to stop and then a gong and a jingle to hook it up ahead. The engine controls were operated from the lower engine room and most engineers or oilers sat on the main deck door sill near the engine room ladder until they got a bell or would see that they were getting close to their destination and amble below. I however, was nervous and stayed right next to the controls and couldn't see where we were or where we were going. Seems like we had to pick up a scow near the Singer Company bulkhead in E Port and there were a lot of pilings jutting out into the waterway from old piers long gone. I didn't know this at the time, couldn't see it and really didn't care. All I could think of was what will the next bell be and will I answer it correctly. The engineer had also told me to be careful of the air pressure in the main tank as air was needed to reverse and start the main engine. If we went low, we had to start the electric air compressor and if that didn't keep up we had to start the 2-71 diesel generator that also ran an air compressor off its front end. So when I started to get bells all these things were going through my mind. My last signal was a jingle; we had been going ahead so I gave the engine full speed. After a few seconds I got a new set of signals, three gongs. Well I knew that two gongs meant to come to a stop but one more gong meant to go ahead half and I didn't think that was right so I went to stop and waited for the anticipated new set of signals but all I got was a jingle. Still not understanding, I just stood there terrified. Then I felt the tug coming to a quick but easy stop as the she ran up on a set of old pier pilings and then felt her sliding off backwards. At the same time I heard the pilothouse door slam and the heavy footfalls of the captain as he made his way down the ladder and then pounding down the deck towards the engine room. The tug was very quiet when nothing was running and the main engine was still stopped. I was scared to death. He stepped into the upper engine room, looked down and saw me, said nothing, turned and started screaming for the engineer. He woke him up and chewed him out for five minutes before going back to the pilothouse. The engineer came below and took over and we completed the pickup of the barge. When we were underway and things calmed down he explained that some captains rang only three bells when they wanted to go from full ahead to astern but that they would swear it wasn't so. Later at the dinner table in the small galley I was sure I would get some flak from the captain but he was nice as could be to me and told me how he knew my father from the steam boats and he hoped I would continue in the tug business because it was honest work and the industry needed young people. He also made a couple of remarks to the engineer about the correct way to train people and how he should try to get some sleep at home before he came to work.

# Chapter 11 - Ellen F. McAllister

One of the tugs I was relief oiler on was the Ellen F. McAllister around 1961/2. She was one of the boats converted to the LST drive at McAllister's Black Tom Yard, with a General Motors 12-567-A main engine, Falk 2 1/2:1 reduction gear with electric/pneumatic controls and a LST bronze propeller. She was long and narrow, a great ship docking tug, but that may have been because of all the great docking pilots that were assigned to her. She was kind of funny looking as she had a pilot house without a Texas house and being so long, seemed out of shape. I had just got on watch at night with the chief so I am not exactly sure where we were, but it was somewhere on the West end of Long Island Sound. We were trying to pull a grounded tanker off some flat somewhere with about four other tugs. We had a relatively short stern line out on the tankers port bow and were pulling towards her stern laying flat against her portside. The ship was working full astern and there were two or three big tugs with hawsers out on her stern. I was standing in the upper engine room on the starboard side because there was nothing to see on the port side as we were right up against the ship. They had being pulling for awhile waiting for the rising tide and still working a half hour into my watch when all of a sudden the tanker slid off like greased lightning. The tug was pulled over as the line we had from our stern to her bow came up tight and pulled us forward and over. I slid across the upper grating and found myself walking on the port side house bulkhead of the upper engine room as we were yanked over and nearly tripped. Thank God the deckhand was experienced and was ready for something like this. He threw a couple of turns off the stern bitts and the rest of the line flew free until it was all paid out.

Being pulled over that fast at that angle I didn't think you would have time to do anything but hang on for dear life. The whole thing was over in 10 seconds. He said later he did it by instinct but barely had time and after he threw the line off he found himself flat on his back sliding down the deck until his feet hit the waist rail and we popped up again. His legs were in water up to his knees. Pots pans, supplies, spares and even the Belgium ballast blocks under the floor plates were strewn all over. Floor plates slid over one another. It happened so quickly and was over so fast we were all asking each other what happened. We had a slight port list until we went to a dock and everyone pitched in to get the Belgium blocks and the floor plates back to where they belonged along with the spares and supplies. Then, back to work. This, I realized was why all floor plates were supposed to be screwed in to the angle iron bracing below. They always were screwed in at the yard but sometimes the crew left the screws out to get to the bilge for maintenance.

# Chapter 12- Dry Docks

Dry docks are a science all to themselves. They are a complicated set of compartments, flooding valves, pumping valves, sluice valves, reach rods, pumps, controllers and deck hardware. Most people only see a dry dock when it is afloat, either with a tug on it or empty. But the skill needed to sink the dock (without actually sinking it!) and then center a tug or barge on it and raise the whole thing without tipping it or having the boat slide off is a real skill. If a wooden dry dock accidently went too deep, the wing wall planks near the top were always dried out and would allow water to rush into the wing wall compartment and the wing walls were where the dock got its stability and flotation when the dock was submerged. This alone could cause the dry dock to sink to the bottom. Luckily there was not always a lot of water under the docks to allow them to completely sink, although it has happened. We had four dry docks at Tug & Barge Dry Docks, Dock 19, Jersey City. Dock 1 was built in the early 1920's, Dock 2 around1925, Dock 3 about 1942 and Dock 4 was built sometime in the 1940's for the Erie RR. We got dock 4 when Erie closed their yard at Pavonia Ave. Jersey City, New Jersey. Years later when I moved the Tug & Barge shipyard from Jersey City behind the Statue of Liberty to Pavonia Avenue in Jersey City, just South of the Holland Tunnel the 4 Dock went right back where she was when Erie Rail Road had it. Two years later I moved her to near the end of the pier so that our tower crane could reach it as well as the other dry docks. George Pillepich was the dock master and carpenter foreman for most of the time I was working at the yard. I have known George since I was 13 years old and first started going to the shipyard with my father. At that time his foreman was Bino. George had come to the U.S. in 1948 from the island Unije that was part of Italy when he was born, then became part of Yugoslavia after WW II and finally part of Croatia. My mother and father went to his wedding. While we were still at Dock 19 JCRR, the original dock master from the Jersey Central crew, George Vickery, was retiring and George Pillepich was sent to Crandall Dry Dock school to become the dock master after a transition period with Vickery. He (Pillepich) was a great craftsman because he came from the old school and old world and was a very conscientious and talented craftsman.

When I took over as General Manager years later he was a little tough to get along with because he remembered me as the kid that he helped break in but along the way became one of my staunchest allies. A dry dock has a set of keel blocks running the length of the center line of the dock and another set of blocks that are pulled in on each side to hold the boat in a stable position as they meet the hull. Chains are attached to the 'pull blocks' and to pulleys near the keel blocks and outboard near the wing wall and then up the side of the wing wall so the dockhands can grab them and pull them in or out. Before sinking the dock the pull blocks are pulled back so they are sitting near the wing wall. When the boat is being docked, it is centered by the dockhands and when it has risen out of the water ever so slightly and the dock master knows that the boat is sitting on the keel blocks he gives the signal to the dockhands to 'pull' the blocks. He does this by yelling through his megaphone to be heard over the noise of the yard machinery and the weather.

The pull blocks would float because they were made of wood but there are 'L' shaped steel brackets wrapped under the stringer they ride on that keep them down and allow them to slide. The chains are then pulled until the blocks hit the hull and the tug is now supported and the pumping out continues until she is up and dry.

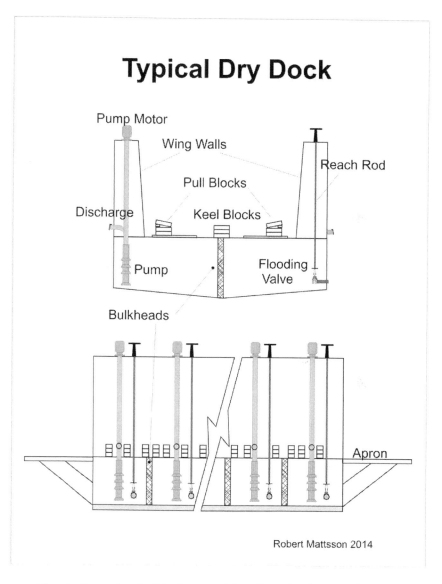

Robert Mattsson 2014

The dock master had to be careful sinking the dock so that it didn't go too far or he could put the wing walls under the water and short out the motors. Coming up you didn't want to stress the dock by pumping out some compartments too fast and open up seams in the planking and then you wouldn't be able to keep up with the pumps. They had to keep water in compartments where there was no vessel weight so the dock wouldn't bend too much. Wooden docks had a lot of give in them, not like steel docks. A problem that occurred occasionally was the reach rods to the valves breaking. This usually meant aborting the dry docking and raising the dock to make the repair.

That reminds me of the time at the Pavonia Avenue yard when a transformer pole was hit by a truck outside our yard. It was a real nasty weather day, blowing and raining and cold, a Nor'Easter. George Pillepich was lowering Dock 2 when we lost the power. Dock 2 had a lot of felt and plywood nailed onto the outside of her wing walls because of leaks in the planking. So without power and leaky wing walls the dock just kept on going down. We had only been at the Pavonia Avenue yard for a short time and the bottom was dredged before we moved the docks up. So there was enough water under her that would allow her to sink altogether before she grounded out. We got pumps from everywhere in the yard and from any of the tugs that also were in the yard. We couldn't stop her though, we slowed it down but she was still slowly sinking. We had just sold the tug Helen McAllister to Eklof Marine, and she was now named the Scandia. She had a 440 volt electrical system, which was the voltage needed for Dock 2's pumps. We called Eklof for help and they got the Scandia underway immediately from Mariners Harbor, Staten Island. Just as the Scandia got there and just as the water was starting to break over the wing walls, the power came back on. The electrician, Urbano, now had to reconnect the power supply as he had disconnected it to get ready to connect to the Scandia. Anyway, power on, dock up, release Scandia and start to put all the pumps and hoses away. Another hairy day. Dock 1 at the Dock 19 facility was another story, she had hardly any water under her and would sit on the bottom when down. We had just enough water over the blocks when she was on the bottom to dock the JCRR Ferries that had a 10' draft. Dock 1 was the only dock the ferries could go on because of their overall width. They were 50' wide with the sponsons jutting out the sides.

As I mentioned previously, Dock 2 had 440 volts for her pumps. My younger brother Carl was an electrician at Tug & Barge for many years and part of his job was maintaining and troubleshooting the electrical equipment on the dry docks. Both my younger brothers, Carl and Mel worked at the yard for years before becoming tugboat engineers. My youngest brother, Bruce was also an engineer for Great Lakes Dredge an Dock Company. Anyway, Carl was checking out a starting box for one of the pump motors high up in the control shack on the outboard wing wall of Dock 2. He was using a volt/ohm meter that was supposed to be good for 440 volts to test the solenoid coils when he felt a jolt come through his meter. Feeling the shock he reached up to the large steel shut off handle on the main power supply. As soon as he did, he became fully grounded, there was a blast, his helper was momentarily blinded as was Carl. Carl went on fire from the inside out. He didn't know it at the time but his hand was burnt and stuck to the shut off handle but he pulled it away and left his skin there. He was screaming and running along the wing wall when my father hearing the electrical blast, came out of his office just in time to see him run off the wing wall. Thankfully, the carpenters were caulking the wing wall planks and had a scaffold rigged just below where he ran off and that's where he fell and lay. It was a good thing it was there or he would have fallen another 15' onto some nasty stuff on the dry dock deck. The whole yard got together and got him down and to the hospital in Jersey City. He had just gotten married and this happened just before Christmas. When I got to the hospital that night, my father and Carl's wife, Julie, were just about in shock. Carl was actually in shock, the skin on his face was burned off as well as the skin on his hands, arms and part of his chest. He couldn't open his eyes and his lips kept sticking together so it was hard to give the sips of water he wanted. Looking at him you thought he was going to die. My father and I didn't think they were doing enough for him and wanted to transfer him to a New York hospital. The doctor came in and said we could do what we wanted but he was doing what he felt was the best thing for him and he promised he would come out of this. The nursing staff was short because of Christmas so they let his wife, Julie, stay in the room with him and keep blotting the ooze draining from his burns. In the end the doctor was right, the only scars really visible years later were on his hands and a faint scar on his face.

The dock master also had to be very careful pumping the port and starboard compartments so the list did not get too severe causing the tug to slip off the blocks. We were putting the Margaret McAllister on Dock 2 when it got away from the dock master and tilted to one side, the Margaret slid off the blocks and for a while it was real scary. I was on the boat and wondered if I should jump over the side. It was pretty scary but George got everything under control quickly and sank the dock as quick as he could and the Margaret came off the blocks and floated upright. Then we started over again, came back on the dry dock and all was fine.

Wooden dry docks had Belgium blocks for ballast so they would sink because they were made of wood, which we all know floats. Steel docks didn't need any ballast. After many years the wooden docks became somewhat water logged and between that and a mud build-up we would go into the compartments and remove some of the Belgium blocks and mud to keep the dry dock buoyant. A real nasty and slippery job. So naturally I was put on that detail. How many people can say they have been on the inside compartments of a dry dock. It was an amazing dark and damp place, loaded with beams and cross braces that gave the deck its strength. We had to pass the Belgium blocks and buckets of mud up through small hatches in the dry dock deck and then trudge it over to a large bucket that the crane could reach and put ashore. George was a master craftsman. I learned a lot about wood, wooden tugs and barges from him as well as cabinetry. He was in charge of all the wood work on the tugs and barges including cap rails, hawser racks, quarters and bunk fabrication, masts and canvas over tongue and groove, not to mention planking, ribs and knees on wooden tugs and barges. The timber came as tree trunks and he and his men would saw it, re-saw it, plane it, rout it and shape it until it was ready for the purpose intended. The saw they used looked like it came right out of the Perils of Pauline. You should have seen him make a hollow round tapered mast from planks. I was always sent as an extra helper when any foreman needed one. This was my father's way of making sure I knew something about each trade. It also kept me from being bored and getting into trouble. One of the jobs I had was putting canvas deck topping over the wood upper decks and line box covers. The skill needed wasn't great but you still had to do it right or you got ripped a new asshole. I would help to stretch the canvas over the wood and after stretching the carpenter and I would double it over and hammer carpet tacks every inch on the seams and where it ended at the fascia. We then coated the canvas with a half and half mixture of green paint and turpentine. When that dried, we put on a coat of plain green paint. When the boat left the yard the crew put on another coat of paint to seal it real well.

    They also taught me how to use an adze and hollow out the bottom of a new rub rail so it would fit tight to the cap rail. If you didn't hollow it out, the bottom sides of the cap rail would open up at the rail proper when the through bolts were tightened. I never got really good at it like the regular carpenters just like I never got really good at caulking like the old timers, but I could do it. It's just that they were much faster at it than I could ever be.

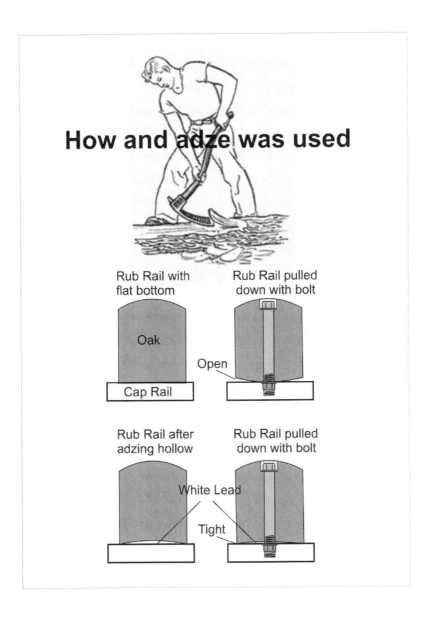

# Chapter 13 - Jersey Central Ferries

When the Jersey Central steam ferries were in the yard we did a lot of work on the main and auxiliary steam engines, the various bearings, the boilers, condensers and valves. Here I learned how to make gaskets from sheet gasket material by placing the material over the pipe or valve flange and tapping the rim with the flat side of a ball peen hammer and making the bolt holes by tapping it with the ball end. Sometimes we would just make the impression on the gasket material with the ball peen hammer if the material was real thick and then cut the circles with a shears and cut the holes with a hole punch. We always brought a 4" x 4" block of hardwood with us when we knew we would be making gaskets. The block was positioned grain up so the surface was hard and not spongy when you hit down on it with the hole punch. We made our own mixture of lube oil and graphite to paint on the gaskets so they wouldn't stick from the heat when we had to remove them again. My teachers were two engineers from the tug Dubois II that worked in the yard during their time off or when the Dubois II was laid up. They were real good guys and terrific engineers. Their names were Joe Dugan & Murphy, I don't think I ever knew Murphy's first name because he was always just called Murphy. These were the same men that taught me how to cut packing the right way. Whether it was 1/4" or

1 1/2". Everyone had a pocket knife in their pocket and we sharpened them every morning on one of the grinding wheels in the machine shop while waiting for our assignments. Everyone thought they had the sharpest knife and wanted to compare theirs with yours. Murphy and Dugan taught me how to wrap the packing around the shaft we were working on and then cut both ends at an angle at one time while it was on the shaft with the sharp knife so the ends would fit together perfectly. On steam equipment we coated the packing with the lube oil and graphite mixture and on water equipment we coated the packing with grease or tallow. Once we had all the pieces cut, we would flatten them slightly with a wooden mallet and insert them into the packing gland. We would put in a few pieces, push it in with a wooden offset tool and then pull it up with the gland, then undo the gland and add the rest. I was warned constantly not to tighten the gland too much because the packing would burn on startup of the machinery. When the piece of machinery was started up later on, we would be there to see if it was leaking too much and felt the gland to see if it was heating up. Then we would tighten or loosen as necessary to have just a very small leak to keep the packing material lubricated. Sometimes we had to add another turn or two.

At the same yard period steel hull work was taking place on dry dock. Large riveted plates that were wasted or thin and condemned by the USCG Inspector were removed by burning out the rivets with oxy-acetylene torches. This was tricky as they had to melt the counter sunk ends back to the rivet shanks without damaging the holes in the frames. After melting and blowing away the outside counter sunk parts of the rivet they were driven out with a hammer and punch. After all the rivets were removed the hull plate was pried off with steel wedges, taken off the dry dock and put in the scrap pile. Templates made with wooden battens were then formed over the area where the plate was removed and sent up to the plate shop. The templates were made from 1/8" x 4" wooden strips called battens and hand fitted into the area where the plate was removed with the ever handy pocket knives and held

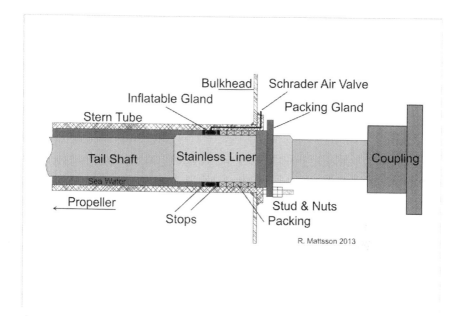

together at the corner by carpet tacks that were just a little too long and when driven through the two pieces being joined would come up against the steel framing and bend over as the iron workers hammered them in. The battens easily bent and took the curved shape of the hull where the old plate was removed. The plate shop positioned the template over a new steel plate, marked it with soap stone and then center punched the outline so the burner could cut it to shape. Then it was manhandled to the area of the punch press and held up by chain falls and maneuvered so the rivet holes could be punched out. The plate might be put under the massive steam hammer at this time to put some shape into it if the needed bend was somewhat severe or compound otherwise it was brought to the dry dock by crane, put down on the dry dock apron deck that stuck out beyond the wing walls and pulled and slid into position near where the plate was going to be put with ropes being pulled by the whole iron working gang and any other trades as needed and then rigged into position with chain falls. Pad eyes were welded to the inside of the new plate and L shaped dogs were welded on adjoining plates outside to hold it in position. Bolts were temporarily put into a few holes and chain falls attached to the pad eyes and to

framing on the inside of the ferry. The chain falls allowed the plate to be pulled into position and take the form of the hull as it was pulled against the framing. As the plate was pulled into place more and more bolts were
employed to keep the plate in position. Then the rivet holes that weren't exactly lined up would be reamed with an air operated reamer just enough that the rivet would fit. Then the hole was reamed again on the outside with a countersink air reamer tool. The rivets going in were usually a little larger in diameter than the ones that were removed because the reaming to align the hole opened the holes up somewhat. The holes were not reamed so much as to make the hole on the framing exactly match with the new plate but just enough to allow the rivet to pass though. Even though the holes were offset the red hot rivets were near melting temperature and would take the shape of the cavity, the offset and the countersink when it was hammered home with the rivet gun. (see insert) When the rivet cooled it would shrink somewhat and make a very tight and water proof joint. At this point the rivet was ringed with a different tool to make sure the flare of the rivet was against the countersunk hole in the new plate. This way the outside of the rivet was flush with the hull so there was no resistance when the ferry was underway. I got to do all the jobs here because it was usually a long operation and helpers were needed. I got to help heat the rivets at a furnace set up on the main car deck. It was a small blast furnace using fuel oil and compressed air to make a very hot
flame that was directed into a furnace that was lined with furnace brick. The receptacle was about 18" x 18" square set up on four legs. You had to anticipate how many and when the rivets were needed so they were hot when ready but not too long in the furnace that they actually melted. When a rivet was needed the riveter would hit th hull with his hammer twice and the holdback man would hit the sheet metal drain pipe that ran from his area to the collection area just above him.

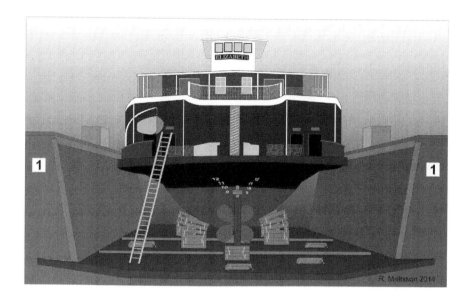

That man, the passer, would rap the drain pipe going up the furnace area. There was a funnel at the beginning of each drain pipe that we would drop the red hot rivet into with tongs and it would drop down the drainpipe and fall into a bucket at the collection area. He would then pick it up with his tongs and drop it into the next drain pipe and it would fall into the bucket of the holdback man. He would quickly pick it up with his tongs and put it into the hole indicated by the riveter and immediately set up his holdback device or shoulder holdback and hit the hull with his hammer when he was ready for the riveter to start mushrooming the exposed rivet. The hold back tool had a cup like cavity that matched the round inside rivet head, known as the factory end. In close quarters the hold back man had a similar gun to the riveter with a cup end tool and when he would start his holdback gun, the riveter outside would start the mushrooming.

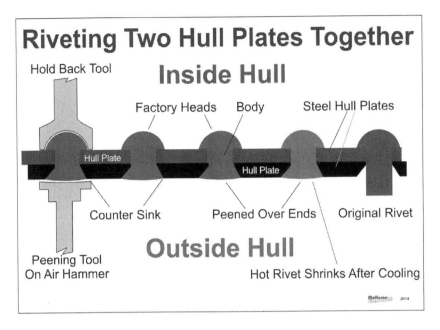

As soon as the rivet was mushroomed the riveter would change tools on the rivet gun to a curved sharp tool and 'ring' the rivet to make sure it was tight to the hull plate and flush. I got to do the hold back a few times and was satisfactory but when I was allowed to go outside and actually rivet, well, that didn't work out too well. I was too slow and being a skinny 18 or 19 year old I didn't have enough beef to lean into it hard enough. So they had to burn out the ones I did. No hard words here, they understood and appreciated that I was trying. The rivet holes in the steel plates were punched in the blacksmith shop on the steam hammer.

    The steam hammer was amazing. It was used to forge pieces, bend steel plate and make pipe clamps, dry dock dogs, steel wedges and of course punching holes in steel. The two guys who worked the hammer and in the blacksmith shop were Paulie and Murphy under the direction of the Iron Worker foreman, Ed Larsen. The steam hammer was at least 12' high and massive and was operated by a long handle connected to the steam valve by Paulie. If you pushed it back the hammer (and its adapter) went up, pull it towards you and it came down. If you pulled or pushed just a little it would move very softly, if you pushed or pulled the handle a lot, it moved very fast and with lots of power. I got to work the steam hammer often as I was friends with Paulie and Murphy. If you were good, you could work the hammer up and down with a small bounce until you were sure where you were going to hit the steel and then give it full power and make your bend, punch or to hit and shape a red hot piece of metal to mold it.

Some years later I was an engineer on the Brian McAllister and I wanted to make a drill press table. I made my sketch and when I got into the yard one day I brought it up to Murphy and Paulie. They thought this was a great project and went right to work on it because they were my friends. Well, there was a hot repair job going on and when Joe Weber, the Superintendent came to the blacksmith shop to find out the progress of this hot job, he found me, Murphy and Paulie working on my project. He went ballistic and wanted to know who was running the ship yard, Joe Weber or Bob Mattsson. He reamed us out and my project had to wait, but it did get done clandestinely a few days later.

After all the dry dock work was finished and approved by the USCG inspector and the hull painted, the ferry was floated off the dry dock and brought alongside the pier to test the machinery and life saving equipment. Now the fun began. As you can imagine, the ferry was needed back on the Manhattan to Jersey City run, the owners and port engineers didn't want to spend any more time or money in the yard and we wanted to get it out on time. To test all the machinery steam was needed. To get the steam engines running we needed USCG steam licensed engineers. This was my father, Arne, the labor foreman, Stoney, who used to be an engineer on these same ferries and the before mentioned engineers from the Dubois II, Dugan and Murphy if they were on their time off and in the yard. Also needed was oilers, wipers and firemen. To actually get the steam up you needed firemen. All engine crew was taken from the yard personnel and one time I was selected to be one of the firemen. Nice job you might say. No. I was given a very large shovel, shown the door to the fire box, shown the coal hopper and told to feed the fire. A whole shovel that size of coal is very heavy and to throw it into the fire box is not easy. To throw it in and have it spread out even is even harder. I would take half a shovel and try to throw it as best and as far as I could but would always end up with a couple of mounds just inside the fire box door. When the real fireman saw how I was doing he would yell to me to spread the coal out. I then had to grab the spreader, a two foot wide piece of flat bar welded to a long pipe and try to push the coal towards the back of the fire box and smooth it out. Then get the shovel again and start to throw more coal in. I was exhausted, hot and muscle sore. The heat was almost unbearable, especially if you had to keep your fire box door open to keep smoothing the coal and shoveling like I did. The real fireman was relaxed and apparently cool as he spread the coal out in one swift and smooth motion with a flick of his shovel. He had a very even and glowing fire all the way to the back of the fire box. Every now and then he would come over to my side and straighten out my fire. I knew him from the tugs and working in the yard but never had the respect for him as I did now. For all coal firemen for that matter. I couldn't wait for this day to end.

During this yard time all the line shaft bearings and main engine bearings on the ferries were blued and scraped. First we put bluing (bluing was just like a dark blue oil paint) on the bearing half shells and turned the engine over with the air operated jacking gear. Then we would remove the shells and scrape the Babbitt with special bearing scraping tools on the high spots where the bluing was wiped off. Then re-blue and do it over again. Sometimes we did it over 10 to 12 times to make sure it was right, especially the propulsion engine main bearings. If these steps were not done right, the Babbitt could melt where it had high spots and possibly seize to the shaft or at least ruin the bearing shell. When everything was thought to be set, all the machinery had steam slowly run through it to warm all the parts up and slowly allowed to rotate or slide. After running slow for awhile all the bearings were felt for heat and the packing's checked during this test period. Then the engines were slowly brought up to speed for the USCG to observe and approve.

When the engine was brought up to speed and all the auxiliary stuff was running plenty of steam was needed. That's when it got hairy in the fire room as noted above. The yard would try to do this part of the inspection after lunch when all the USCG Inspectors and Port Engineers came back full from their meal and had a few drinks under their belt. This way they were more apt to overlook small discrepancies.

This happened one afternoon when we were checking the life saving equipment. One of the standard checks were the lifeboats. They would put as many yard workers in a lifeboat as was stated on her builders capacity plaque to check her buoyancy and stability. My co-workers and I were in the boat laying alongside the ferry with two lines out so the USCG Inspector could see that all was right when I noticed a leak. I got on my knees and saw that two rivets holding the galvanized steel sheets together under the seat bench were missing and water was squirting in. I yelled to Joe Weber, the superintendent that we had a leak. The Inspector had turned away and didn't notice but Weber put his finger to his lips, indicating I should be quiet. But being me, I said again that we had a leak. I could see he was burning up and he came to the rail, leaned over and quietly told me to shut up. I said "But it's a lifeboat, suppose it's really needed". He gave me a dirty look and promised we would fix it later. Later did come the next day and guess who got to climb under the lifeboat seat bench and install the new rivets with a helper outside to peen them over? Oh well, another learning experience.

# Chapter 14 - Wheel Gang

I also worked on the wheel gang a lot. The specialties of the wheel gang was changing out propellers, unshipping and replacing rudders, pintle bushings, steering quadrants, steering chains and cables and removing and replacing tail shafts as well as any big rigging jobs. Each tug, fishing boat and ferry had their peculiarities. Some had bronze propellers, some had stainless steel propellers and some had cast iron propellers. Some propellers had three blades, some four blades and some five blades. Then on others there was the variable pitch propellers with complicated hubs. On some boats the rudder had to be removed to remove the propeller, on others you had to disconnect the steering to get the rudder extremely hard over to get the propeller on and off and still others that only had to have the rudder turned over to one side. Now, in order to do all this removing and installing, two to five chain falls might be needed. Some of the newer boats had permanent pad eyes welded to the hull to expedite things but on most boats the iron workers had to weld pad eyes as directed by the wheel gang foreman to hang the chain falls. Most of these pad eyes were burned off at the completion of the job. Some boats had fuel tanks aft or riveted seams or maybe just very thin hull plates and we couldn't weld anything to the hull. Or maybe there was no time to wait for the welder. In that case we

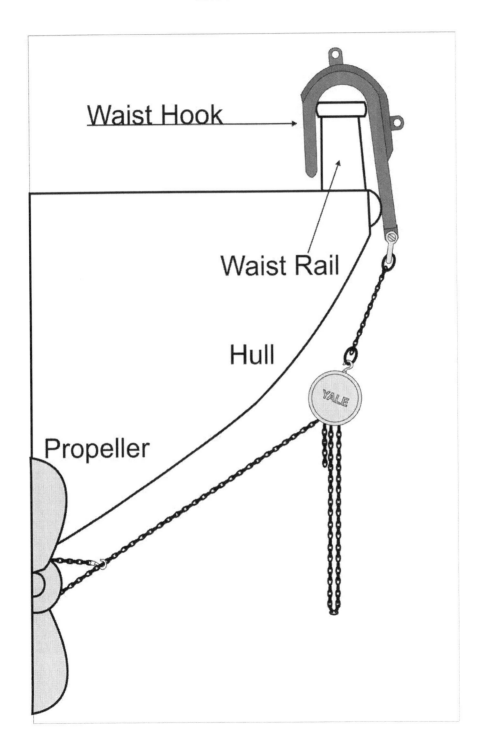

used a device called a waist hook. The hook had pad eyes that we shackled in a piece of line to pull it up into place on the tugs railing and to lower it to the dry dock deck when we were finished. You can see the pad eyes in the diagram. There was one for each side, port and starboard. To install the propellers they were expanded with heat and shrunk onto the tail shaft taper. The same heating procedure was used to remove the propeller. Different material propellers were heated differently because of their expansion rates. Bronze expanded the most and the quickest and could take the most heat without damage to the hub. Stainless steel could not take extreme heat without checking in the metal of the hub so the 2 oil torch was held a little further away from the propeller so it would heat slower and took a little more time. The cast iron propeller was even more fragile when heating so a very slow warm up was

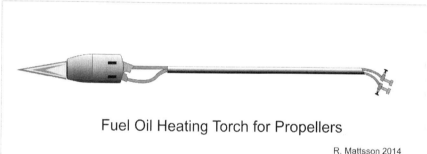

Fuel Oil Heating Torch for Propellers

R. Mattsson 2014

needed. To light the oil torch we would dip a rag in 2 oil, light it and rest the torch head on the flaming rag. When we thought it was hot enough we opened the fuel valve from the pressurized oil tank and when it ignited we opened the air valve to the nozzle and regulated the flame with the fuel and air valves so it was hot and constant. Then the heat was applied to the

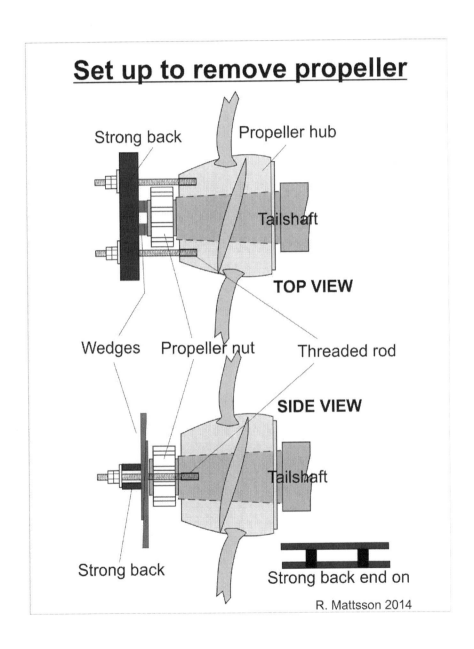

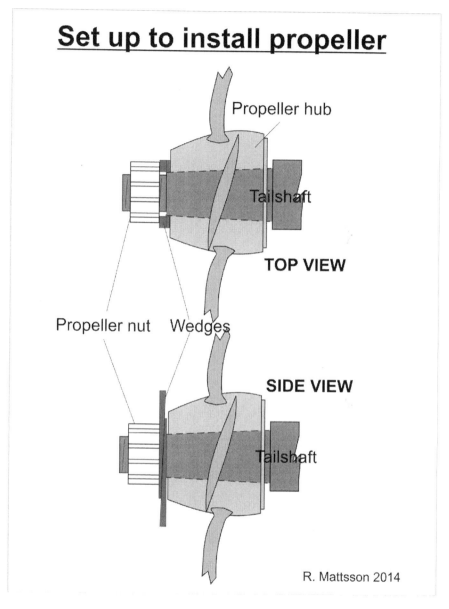

propeller hub. In the mean time the propeller was set up for pulling off or pressing on with the propeller nut, threaded rod and steel wedges made for this purpose. The wedges had a real shallow taper. After the appropriate time (depending on the material and size of the hub) the torch was shut off and the heat allowed to penetrate the hub for three to five minutes. Then the wedges were struck with a 20 pound sledge hammer until the propeller was driven up the tail shaft taper at least 1/8" and close to 3/16" or if removing the propeller until it popped off the taper. On the Jersey Central ferries we not only changed the propellers and shafts but made repairs to the cast iron wheels or propellers. Cavitation sometimes made some of the cast iron of the propeller eat away near the hub and left holes as deep as three inches. We mixed a cement called water plug and forced this into the holes and smoothed it out. I thought this was crazy. However, years later I would get to see what we had done and it was still holding up.

Many of the McAllister boys would work in the yard or on the tugs during their summer break from college. They all worked hard and were not afraid to get down and dirty. That reminds me, one summer we had the President of McAllister at the time, Ed Todd, send his nephew to the yard for summer college break. I worked alongside him using air powered chisels to remove the asphalt under the rails on a Jersey Central car float to get ready for sand blasting and epoxy paint. He worked as hard as anyone else in the summer heat and dust we created and never complained. He only weighed

about 120 pounds soaking wet then. One day the wheel gang needed helpers and he and I were selected. I liked him and wouldn't have set him up but the guys had their rituals and he was their target today. After getting the strong back and wedges in place to pull a propeller but before the heat was applied, the wedges were driven up tight with a 20 pound sledge hammer. They had me and others do this before and told us to hit the top of the wedges as hard as we could with the sledge hammer. Most of us missed the wedges and hit the scaffolding planks with a bang. This caused much hilarity and hazing from the regular wheel gang guys. Others brought the sledge hammer back as fast and as hard as they could and it would fly out of their hands, again creating lots of laughter and embarrassment to whoever swung the hammer. Well, when Todd's nephew got the hammer, I think he knew something was up and he wasn't going to embarrass himself. So when they told him to hit the wedges with all he had, he brought the sledge hammer back as fast and as strong as he could. Well the weight of the 20 pound sledge was too much and he should have let go when he brought it back but he was so determined he held on and he and the hammer went flying off the scaffolding planks. Luckily it was only a thee foot drop so he wasn't seriously hurt. We all rushed to help him and there was no laughing as we got him up. He got some respect after that from the guys. We became summer buddies because we got a lot of the crap jobs together and enjoyed working with each other.

# Chapter 15 - Asbestos

At all engine overhauls in the ship yard, one of the first jobs was to cut off the lead and aluminum painted canvas that covered the exhaust manifolds. We did this with our always handy pocket knives and then removed the baling wire with diagonal wire cutting pliers. We used hand saws and hammers to cut and break off the asbestos blocks, picked up the larger pieces, carried them up to the after deck in our arms and threw them into a yard box. Then we swept up the small pieces and the dust and put it in plastic bags and brought them to the same dump box. This was done first to prevent any of the asbestos dust from getting into the engine cylinders or crankcase during the overhaul. After the overhaul when the manifold and exhaust pipes were put back in place, we cut new pieces from semi-circular asbestos blocks with hand saws, held the blocks in place with baling wire and filled the cracks between the blocks with dry asbestos fibers mixed with water to make an asbestos paste and filled the cracks or openings. All this got into our noses and throats and made our skin itch. We treated this as normal ship yard work. Then we fitted the new canvas around the asbestos that was wired in place and sewed it up tight. Then the whole thing was painted with aluminum paint. In the wheel gang we also mixed dry asbestos with water using our hands and or a wooden paddle. Then we placed the mixture around the opening between the propeller and the stern bearing proper to prevent melting of the rubber on a rubber cutless bearing or the soft metal on a Babbitt bearing or burning the lignum vitae of the wood bearings while heating the propeller with the very hot 2 oil torches used while removing or installing the propellers. I would say almost all of the gasket material we used had asbestos as an ingredient also. Probably the worst offender of asbestos dust was the generator exhaust pipes. The generators vibrated a lot and this was transferred to the exhaust pipe and shook the now very dry asbestos loose. Sometimes it looked like it was snowing. Did we or anybody else worry about this? Actually no, we took it for granted that it was a normal ship yard procedure. At that time no one knew it could harm you.

# Chapter 16 - Stern Bearings

Stern Bearings were made of Babbitt, a relatively soft metal or lignum vitae that was a special wood from Africa that didn't expand much in water and had special lubricating qualities, and cutlass or special rubber material. Babbitt bearings were lubricated with oil and needed special seals to prevent losing the oil to the sea and to prevent water from coming in that could ruin the bearing. Rubber cutlass bearings and lignum vitae were lubricated with water that was either pumped in via the main engine raw water pump, special pumps for that purpose or scoops on the external stern tube. The bearing had longitudinal grooves that not only allowed the water to cool and lubricate the bearing but wash out any sand or mud picked up while operating in shallow water. Sometimes aligning the stern bearing required boring the stern tube and ordering oversized brass cutlass bearings to fit the new bore. The alignment and boring could take from 4 to 8 days and then we had to fit the bearing shell. This required exact measurements of the bore by the inside machinists so they could machine the outside diameter of the bearing. There were usually three separate steps machined in the stern tube that the brass outer shell of the new (or rebuilt) bearing had to match up with. Temperature was a factor as the bearing just after machining was warm and the metal was slightly expanded. So after cooling and brought to the dry dock a test fit was made with bluing and usually brought back for another skim cut. It was easier to remove a little metal from the bearing shell than to put it back on of course. Although on some bearings that is exactly what we did. For bronze shell bearings we used a procedure known as metal spraying.

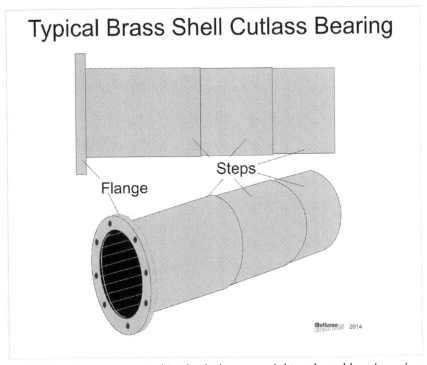

As the bearing was rotated in the lathe a special torch and brazing wire feed was connected to the lathe horizontal feed and a metal coating was sprayed onto the surface of the bearing. After cooling the bearing was machined to size. If there was a very large difference between the bore and the bearing which happened when we used a bearing from another tug with the same inside dimensions but much smaller outside dimensions we would machine sleeves to shrink over the shell steps. The sleeves were slightly under sized so they were warmed up and slid over the shell. When they cooled, they shrunk and were tight to the bearing shell. Then the outside diameter was machined to fit the bore as above. All this took a great deal of time. After a few years we learned a new way to do this. We would cut holes in the stern tube or strut with a torch or drill a hole in the top and bottom of the stern tube and fit pipes into it either by tapping threads or welding the pipes to the stern tube holes we just made and pour an epoxy product called Chock Fast into the stern tube. This would fill the void between the stern tube bore and the stern bearing shell. The Chock Fast was poured into the pipe that was connected to the bottom of the stern tube. This pipe had fittings and a length of pipe that brought it above the top of the stern tube. The top hole on the stern tube had a short length of pipe connected to it. This was the vent and when the chock fast began to come out of the vent we knew the area was filled with the product. We machined 3/16" off the diameter of the cutlass bearing brass shell, aligned the bearing in the normal way, sealed the ends with foam rubber and/or a moldable clay like material and poured the Chock Fast. An hour later it was hard as a rock and ready to go.

Robert Mattsson

## Chapter - 17  Wm. H. McAllister

I was the oiler on the canal tug Wm. H. McAllister when I was around 19 or 20. All the guys on her were much older than me. The Wm. H. was pilothouse controlled so the oiler usually worked the chief's watch and on some boats we worked the day watch, 6 AM to 12 noon and then noon to 6 PM with a break for lunch. My job was to check all fluid levels and add as necessary, sluice the steering cables with heavy grease, sand and stone the commutators on all the DC motors and generators, clean the fire box on the galley stove once a week, clean the soot from the galley and heating furnace stacks, wipe down the engines every watch, wash the floor plates once a week or more and did a lot of painting. The worst job was cleaning the main engine air boxes. This was the part of the engine where the air from the Roots blowers was introduced into the cylinder ports. They were full of a black sooty grit and a tar like coating. This job had to be done when shut down of course so we didn't always get the chance to finish the whole job all at once. We would use rags dipped in fuel oil and a scraper to remove the black gritty paste. I would put the gritty soot into a bucket that was sitting on the floor plates that was lined with newspaper to try and keep it off the floor plates. The stuff would get ingrained in your skin and nails so you hoped you didn't have to do it near the end of your time on because it took two or three days to wash off. The oiler was also expected to help the deckhand put out and take in the pushing gear and handle the stern lines when necessary. Another weekly job was to blow out, clean and replace any worn carbon discs on the carbon pile regulators that kept the DC voltage more or less constant. This was before solid state regulators. And many other regular chores, like making sure the bilge was pumped, keeping the tail shaft packing gland tight but still dripping just a bit, keeping the governor oil level at the mark on the glass (they leaked a lot), draining air tanks of water that condensed in them once a day and keeping the little felt filters on the air compressor un-loaders clean. Once a week we would check all the contacts in the starting boxes and clean, sand, file or replace as necessary, particularly the steering gear as there wasn't any redundancy on that.

Some couple of years later I was working on my time off at Tug & Barge Ship Yard and was assigned to the Wm. H. overhaul. I remember the overhaul was kind of special. We didn't just do the main engine, which is where I was assigned most days but the yard redid the galley floor and the linoleum on the galley table, lots of paint and steering gear maintenance, redid the exhaust lagging (asbestos) and overhauled the auxiliary generator as well as changed out the shaft generator. She was dry docked and a reconditioned propeller was fit and the hull painted. The deck crew came back early to paint the house and deck. I remember when she left the yard we were all proud and she looked real good. Some of the canal guys who were working in the yard for the winter when their boats were laid up were jealous it wasn't their boats turn. Unfortunately, that fall, November the 17th of 1963, on the way back from Burlington, Vermont pushing a light Gulf Oil Company barge she ran into Schuyler Reef on Lake Champlain and sunk in deep water. The crew all walked off onto the barge before the pushing gear let go and she went to the bottom. No one was injured and the tug was never raised.

# Chapter 18 - Eileen McAllister

The Eileen McAllister was originally the 'Adriatic', Official Number 204816. She was a Steel steam screw tug built 1907 at Philadelphia by Neafie & Levy (earlier ABS Record's say J. H. Dialogue & Sons) for P.F. Martin, Philadelphia. 78' x 20' x 10'; 113 gt, 76 nt; single-cylinder steam engine, 18 x 20, 300 ihp, built by builders; one return-tube boiler, 9 x 13,' 125 psi wp. Transferred to Martug Towing Company in mid-'30s. To Stanwood Towing Company (McAllister), 1950. Renamed 'Eileen McAllister', repowered and rebuilt 1952:78' x 20' x 10'; 121 gt, 82 nt; one 12-cylinder EMD Diesel, 8.5 x 10, 1000 bhp. Transferred to McAllister Bros., Inc., 1953.

## Pea Soup

McAllister Brothers Towing had a policy of only using engineers with a United States Coast Guard issued engineers license, unless of course, it suited them. I was studying for my license and was employed as an oiler on the Teresa McAllister when an engineer was needed in an emergency on the 1000 HP canal tug Eileen McAllister. She was the one with port lights for pilothouse windows installed at McAllister's old Black Tom repair yard. I was called at home on my time off by the port engineer and told to call in that night and report as engineer on the Eileen the next day.

This was a real break because my seniority as an engineer would begin the day I was officially entered into the boat's log as an engineer. Besides that, I was excited that Red Edmunds, the Port Engineer had enough faith in my abilities to give me the opportunity. That evening I called the McAllister dispatcher and started to proudly tell him that I was the relief engineer for the Eileen when he cut me off and said "Pier 13, North River, noon tomorrow" and hung up. I guess he wasn't as excited as I was.

Being relatively new and reporting for my first job as an engineer I was nervous and excited and arrived at Pier 13 at eleven o'clock in the morning to make sure I would be on time. It was a cold and windy day in December with the wind and the rain coming out of the Northeast and a heavy chop out in the bay. I kept looking for the Eileen down the bay and up the river because I didn't know where she would be coming from. She had a very low pilothouse with portholes as pilothouse windows and was hard to see even in normal conditions but she wasn't in sight and I was afraid to go back inside the pier for fear of missing her and the crew change.

When I left home in the morning I had my small carry bag with my toilet articles, socks, work shoes and work clothes but I did not bring any heavy weather gear as I was only a relief engineer and didn't want to carry too much back and forth. The dress coat I was wearing to get from Staten Island to Manhattan and then to Pier 13 was not a heavy coat and now with the rain and the wind I was becoming extremely cold. I thought of walking back through the pier to the street to try and find a pay phone to call in. The pier itself was all of 800 feet long and hadn't been used for a long time and I didn't know how far I would have to go in the West Street area to find a working pay telephone. I felt if I left the pier to make the call to the dispatchers the boat would surely show up and I would miss my crew change and possibly the job.

By 12:30 in the afternoon I was very anxious, very cold and very hungry. The Eileen was nowhere in sight and if anything it seemed to be blowing harder and getting colder. I began to think I was at the wrong place because I could not believe the boat would be this late. By one o'clock I was a real wreck, I thought for sure I was in the wrong place but I just knew if I left this spot the tug would magically appear and I would lose the engineer position. I tried to keep to the southern side of the pier in one of the cargo door setbacks but it seemed an eddy would form and find me no matter where I went. One thirty in the afternoon and no boat. I was positive of two things. One, if I left the pier she would surely show, because how late could she be? The other that I was in the wrong place and should beat it up the pier, find a telephone and find out where I was really supposed to be.

I was still weighing the problem at ten minutes to two o'clock when I seemed to see something low moving north off of Bedloe's Island. What I saw was mostly spray but I knew there had to be a boat behind there somewhere. Two o'clock, it was definitely the Eileen and she cutting across the river heading directly for my little spot of hell. The tide was out and the closer she got the smaller and lower she looked. The tide and current were at the last of the ebb and the guy steering knew how to handle a boat. Later I learned he was one of the infamous Frenchy brothers "Ozzie LaFontaine". It seemed like he came to within 10 feet of the pier head before he clutched out, stemmed the tide with a little right rudder and came into the fender piles with a small bump and stuck like a magnet. The deckhand yelled to me to throw my bag and jump down. It looked like quite a ways down and I was expecting a ladder but I was young, so I threw the bag and jumped. I didn't just fall straight but crouched my legs and spread out my arms to take the shock. Before I could even straighten out the captain gave her left rudder and full ahead and we were out of there. He was good. I looked around for my bag but the deckhand had already thrown it into the galley and across the floor. I entered the galley through the starboard watertight door and the cook who I had never met before yelled, "sit here" while pointing to a stool near the port door. There were no interior doors except for a small opening to the pilothouse, forward and over to the starboard side. The galley was small and dark as there were only two small portholes. Most D.C. boats tried to keep un-needed lights off in the daytime so the shaft generator could charge the batteries. The table was small with four small stools around it. The standard issue red and white checkered tablecloth was on the table and there was only one setting, mine. The cook without so much as a 'how do you do' plopped a steaming hot bowl of pea soup down in front of me. Now, my mother made pea soup all the time (she was Irish) and I would never eat it. I couldn't stand the smell or the looks of it. Pale green and thick with lumps of ham didn't look like something one should eat. Actually, it looks a lot like vomit. Well, I was starving and I was cold through, so I ate it and whatever came after it. While I was still eating the engineer came in and said he had been up for over 18 hours and was hitting the sack. My jaw dropped because I had never worked on this tug while it was operating although I had been on her during overhaul at McAllister's yard at Dock 19, Jersey Central Railroad. He didn't notice or care about my obvious distress but went to his bunk. I gobbled down the rest of the meal, thanked the cook and headed for the engine room without changing my clothes.

For the next three and a half hours I just stared at the gauges, the thermocouples, felt the shaft bearings, checked the stern gland, the bilges and the switchboard hoping nothing would go wrong or get hot or run out of fuel. Well, luckily, nothing did go wrong. I investigated all the nicks and crannies of that small engine room and when I was relieved at 6 o'clock by the engineer, it was with profound relief and also pride that I had stood a watch (half a watch) as an engineer. It ended up being a great crew, great boat, good experience and...I have loved pea soup ever since!

On the Eileen we had a small toilet in a very small compartment on the starboard side about 3' x 2 1/2' with only the outside water tight door for access. The toilet sat on a pipe that went directly overboard. There was a check valve at the hull but the flapper was either wasted or gone altogether. There was the watertight door you closed when you got in and a push button to ring a bell in the pilot house if you wanted to get out and the weather and waves were beating up against the door. The head was just aft of amidships and there was no freeboard here. So if you wanted out and the waves were coming over the rail you pushed the bell button that rang in the pilot house and when the captain or mate decided it was safe he would turn the tug (and tow) so the starboard side was more or less in the lee and blow the peep whistle. Sometimes you had to wait five minutes or more. You had to be quick because almost as soon as he did turn the tug so we had the lee, he blew two whistles telling you he was coming back on course. I would run to the after bitts on the stern and then make my way up the port side to the engine room door, usually with wet feet. One time I was sitting on the toilet and we went through a Staten Island ferry wake in the harbor. The wake sucked the water out of the overboard pipe and then sent a gush of water back up and nearly knocked me off the toilet. I was soaking wet and mad as hell! When I told the crew they just laughed at me. It seems they all had the same experience at one time or another.

I'm going to guess this is the picture of Ozzie LaFontaine in his mid 50's. He has his hand on the old LST throttle control with the bicycle grip on it and you can see one spoke of the steering wheel in the foreground. He is looking out of an open pilothouse port.

If you look just above his head you can see the port light swung up in its stowed position not far from his head and he wasn't a tall man. Besides bumping your head on them, every now and then, particularly when backing they would vibrate off their hangers and come down with authority. They were not light by any means. A natural thing to do was to put your hand at the bottom of the port and/or stick your head out slightly to see better and naturally, that is when they fell. It was a real problem and was finally remedied by moving the anchor points of the hangers forwards towards the port lights so they were at an extreme angle and were hard to release. No easy job as they had to remove the overhead and burn off and re-weld the anchor points in the ship yard.

## Chapter 19 - The Three Copper Cigars

"794 to the Eileen, come in on the Eileen". The McAllister Towing Company night dispatcher was calling the canal boat Eileen McAllister. He repeated the message because they always did and the pilothouse people never answered the first call anyway. This was over the big blue RCA, VHF radio that took up a large portion of the shelf at the back of the pilothouse. It was a warm evening in August, sometime around 1961. "Eileen back" the mate said as he keyed the mike. He hoped the next job would send us on our way to the canal with an oil barge instead of the New York Harbor work we had been doing for the last couple of days. Regular canal Captains/Mates were not too fond of the harbor and much preferred the New York State Barge Canal work to the hectic pace of the local harbor work. Here in the harbor it was nonstop, always a new tow or shift or helping on a ship job. Derrick barges, coffee barges, railroad barges, car floats, oil barges, deck scows, scrap barges, copper barges, ammo barges (overtime, actually double-time, so not looked down on too much), shifting at the fruit, coffee, railroad or general cargo piers. Sometimes shifting mud scows but thank God never towing them to sea. We were way too small for that. Always something, hardly ever "hangin' on". And even worse was the chance they would be ordered to do a tough ship assist. We were small but still just a tug to the dispatchers so they would try to give us any assignment even if it really required a bigger tug and would berate the Captain if he tried to get out of the job or asked for a helper tug. " Eileen, you have two copper boats out of Raritan going to Yonkers, they are ready now" said the dispatcher. "Pick up the Gillen 25 and the Manhattan 15 for delivery to Phelps Dodge as soon as possible". We were at Gulfport Staten Island, N.Y., so that was about a 30 minute trip if the Raritan railroad bridge opened when we got there. Rounding the bend at Perth Amboy the mate blew the three long blasts on the whistle to notify the bridge we wanted to get through. The bridge answered with three so we knew he would be opening. Just past the bridge on our right or north side was the copper dock. The 25 and the 15 were inside four other barges so we had to do some shifting to get them out and ready to tow.

The dock people were there to tell us exactly how they wanted the light barges lined up for loading. This was a free shift for them. When the deckhand saw how much shifting was involved he started to complain and the mate said "okay, okay, break the oiler out to help you". I never refused overtime. The deckhand and I made all the required moves and finally got the two barges alongside, one ahead of the other, and left the pier. We went past the still open Raritan River Railroad Bridge and headed up the Kills for the Hudson River and Yonkers. Just like we did after almost every tough job we all met in the Eileen's tiny pilothouse with fresh coffee and a supply of cigarettes. When I was a young fella, early to late 60's, everyone smoked, including the cook. Yes, we had cooks. Pilothouses had at least six ashtrays. I am not condoning smoking mind you. Bad for your health they tell me. But boy, did we smoke and drink coffee. Always a pot on and sometimes two. Ashtrays made from almost anything you could think of, shells (both kinds), pistons, coffee cans, soup cans, coiled copper tubing, hammered sheet metal, you name it. Another thing, if we washed the coffee pot with soap we caught holy hell. It could only be rinsed. The pilothouse at night on a long tow is a quiet place to reflect, to dream, to talk of family and fantasy. The engineer came up also after awhile and we began to talk about the value of the cargo on the barges. Copper cigars or ingots weighed about 200 pounds each. They were stacked on the barge in groups of five across and five across perpendicular on top of that for about five layers. The stacks on the barge totaled about 40 so we figured the value was about $200,000., a lot of money. We wondered how they kept track of all this. Did they know how many bars were on board? Would they miss a couple? Did Raritan tell Yonkers how many were coming up on the barge? What was the value of one bar at the scrap dealer? Would the scrap dealer take it? We kept going round and round on the subject. The value of copper scrap at the time was .65/pound. That would be $130 for each bar. This was a lot of money in the 1960's. "The scrap dealer wouldn't take it though" said the engineer. "Yeah, we would have to cut it up into small pieces said the mate". "A lot of work" said I. Nothing was said for a long time as we made our way up past Elizabeth Port in New Jersey and then Port Richmond, Staten Island in the dark, just looking at the shore lights, not saying much when the deckhand broke the silence off Saint George and said "we could get in big trouble if we were caught". Yeah... but how will we get caught I said. "Especially if we cut it up".

Well, one thing led to another and before you know it the whole crew is out lugging copper bars to the engine room. It wasn't easy, the shape and weight didn't lend them well to carrying. They were about 4 foot long, 5 inches across at the center and tapering to about 3 inches near the ends. They looked like big cigars. After struggling half the night three bars were brought down into the engine room. They were heavy and tying a rope sling around them was tough because the bars had a tendency to slide out of our knots. The dispatcher called and wanted to know when we would land the barges because the oil barge Manhasset was almost topped off at Gulfport and was going to Rensselaer, near Albany, N.Y. We couldn't make it back in time so the Ellen F. McAllister was sent to pick the Manhasset up, bring her up the Hudson and pass her off to us. That suited us just fine. I set up one of the cigars up on the work bench and began to cut a three inch piece off the end with a hacksaw. Two hours later with sore arms and only halfway through, I gave up and went to my bunk for some rest before the 5:30 am wake up call. The copper barges were dropped off and the Eileen headed south to meet the Ellen F. The Ellen F. had the barge alongside so we came around and went into the pushing notch at the stern of the barge and put out the pushing gear and safety lines. We traded some books with the Ellen F. crew and let their lines go. By this time it was mid morning and a bright clear day. Later, when the mate got off watch and came to lunch he remarked that the New York City police boat had been behind us for two hours. No one thought much about it and even later when we saw police helicopters over us a couple of times as we headed up the river we didn't give it a second thought. We were getting ready to land at Gulf Rensselaer the next morning when the deckhand said we had better hide the bars because today was crew change day and we didn't want anyone to know what we had. It was decided to put the bars in the bilge under the deck plates and to continue cutting them up when we came back in a week. We landed the barge and the dock man said there were some guys in suits asking about the tug a little earlier.

    We let go of the Manhasset and made our way up to McAllister's dock which was really just two sets of piles near the shore at Rensselaer and put our lines out. Up on the bank were the McAllister runner, the relief mate who lived local and three guys in dark suits. Nobody looked happy. We still hadn't put it all together so we went about our business tying up and shutting down. When the board that served as a gangway was put out everyone but the mate came aboard. We were told to get everyone together in the galley but when they saw how small it was we were herded to the stern. When we were all gathered the men introduced themselves as FBI agents and asked us where the copper ingots were. Well, you could have blown us over. All kinds of emotions went over us, surprise, fear, remorse, shock, terror. No one could speak, no one wanted to speak. The men asked again "Okay guys, where are the copper bars you took from the barge yesterday?" Realizing we were caught the mate said they were in the engine room bilge. We were made to take them out, bring them up on deck and lug them up to the agent's cars on the bank. Then we sat down individually with the agents and gave up all our personal information, including USCG License numbers for those that had them. This was scary. There were a lot of calls to the copper plant, McAllister's New York office and the New York FBI office. All this took time because they had to keep going up to the runner's office where the telephone was and then back down to the boat. We really didn't care anymore though because we figured we were going to jail for a long time anyway. The relief crew had all arrived by now but weren't allowed on board.

The Peter B. McAllister tried to come alongside to tie up but they were waved away and told to hang on over at the Albany wall. We should have been home by now, it was getting late and we hadn't been allowed to call our families. After what seemed like forever, the agents (now with some NYS Troopers) gathered us all together and after chewing us out and warning of severe consequences if anything like this happened in the future. They told us the copper company was not going to press charges, McAllister was going to put a note in our file but we were not fired and we were free to go home! We were so relieved we felt like crying but held it in. Later, on the train to the New York City we got together and after a few minutes of babbling we were all very quiet. We expected to get a good ribbing from the other crews and we did for years to come but I guess we deserved it.

# Chapter 20 - Steering on the Hudson

Another time on the Eileen McAllister we were coming down the Hudson River towing an oil barge on short gate lines behind us and the two LaFontaine's and the engineer were playing cards in the galley. The deckhand was steering but they wanted him in the galley to play poker and get some of his money. I wouldn't play because I didn't have money to lose so they put me in the pilot house and told me to steer towards a certain point. I was pretty green at this time. When I got close to the point they told me to go to, I was to blow once on the peep whistle and they would come up and give me another point to steer for. This went on for awhile and the last point they gave was to the center of a bridge in the distance. I thought I was doing well and started to get comfortable when all of a sudden we went up a sand or mud bar in shallow water and stopped. I didn't have to notify anyone as I could hear them scrambling to get to the pilot house. They were too late. The barge came up and hit us in the stern, pushed the stern down and the tug forward and we were free again and although the bow was forced to starboard we straightened out pretty quick. It all happened so fast that I hadn't touched the throttle so we got away from the barge almost right away. The bow rake of the barge took out the after boat deck railing, the search light and the flag pole but otherwise, no serious damage. No one blamed me and we were able to make the repairs later by ourselves so no one ever found out.

# Chapter 21 - Winter Watchman

One winter weekend the Eileen tied up at Dock 19 Jersey City and I was called by Mr. Edmunds to watch her and a few other boats over the weekend. I was happy to get the job, even though it was on my time off. I was to be at the yard by 8:00 am and got up at 6:30 to leave at 7:00. There had been a heavy snow fall overnight and the roads were covered with about 4 to 6 inches of heavy snow. My father was lending me his 1951 Chevy wagon to get to work and I left right on time. By the time I got to the end of Mountainview Avenue which was my street, the car wasn't handling right. I crossed Victory Boulevard and had trouble maneuvering. I pulled over and discovered I had a flat. In the falling snow and in the freezing cold I managed to change the tire and got underway again. After about 50 feet the car had trouble maneuvering again. I got out and sure enough the tire I had just changed was flat. I called my father from the corner store and he said he would come get the car later but I should get on the bus and get to work. Well, to get to Jersey City from Staten Island was no easy trick at that time. I waited for a bus to get to the Staten Island Ferry and after a half hour I realized they weren't running. I started to hitchhike and finally got a ride on an oil delivery truck that took me most of the way to Saint George. I walked the rest of the way to the Saint George Ferry Terminal and took the ferry to the Battery in Manhattan. From there I trudged in the snow to the West side and took the Central Rail Road of New Jersey ferry over to Jersey City.

At the Ferry Terminal that was also the Jersey Central Rail Road Station, I went to the coffee counter and asked for two hamburgers, uncooked so I could make lunch and dinner later. The counter girl didn't want to give them to me but after I explained my situation and she observed that I was freezing, she relented and bagged the burgers and rolls separately for me. To go around the rail yards the way the streets did would have been a big undertaking in the snow covered roads so I decided to cut across the rail yards the way I heard some of the yard workers did when they missed the truck that was used to transport them to the yard. I myself had never gone this way before. When I started out it looked like a snow covered plain. Smooth with little humps and bumps. I soon found the humps were little depressions between tracks and the bumps were the rail tracks. I tripped and fell at least 10 times and was cold and wet. I wasn't dressed for an arctic exposition as I expected to drive right to the yard. As I got close and could see the coal dumping machines on Dock 18 I picked up my pace.

There was a long hollow in front of me and I thought it was shallow dip between tracks. I was moving along at a good pace when all of a sudden I was sliding down into complete darkness. I twisted around and headed for what I hoped was up on my hands and knees as fast as I could go. I could see light and was so happy even though I was covered in snow. I made my way out and realized I left my bag of burgers at the bottom. That's where they stayed. I made my way around to where I could see that there was some level ground and made my way to the tug. From there I went to the Watchman's shack and he let me use the phone to call my father. When I got him he told me that Mr. Edmunds had called and said I didn't have to go to work in this snow storm! I stayed the whole weekend and finally warmed up. I went home Monday afternoon with my father. I think he was proud that I got to my job even though he didn't say so.

# Chapter 22 - Margaret McAllister

After a few relief jobs and the stint on the Eileen McAllister I was told to report to the Margaret M. McAllister because the chief was so tough he couldn't keep an oiler. As a matter of fact he had just fired his son-in-law. The Margaret M. McAllister was originally the W. J. Harahan, Steel single screw tug built 1928 at Newport News, VA, by Newport News SB&DDCo. as hull no. 327 for the Chesapeake & Ohio RYCo., Richmond, VA. 102.8' x 28.1' x 13.6'; 266 gt, 134 nt; F & A HP steam engine, 20-44 x 30, by builders, 800-ihp. Sold 1949 to McAllister Bros., Inc., and renamed Margaret M. McAllister. Repowered in 1958 with a 16-cylinder Cleveland Diesel, 8.75 x 10.5, 1800-bhp, built 1945.

This is the conversion I wrote about earlier. The entire conversion was done at Tug & Barge's Pier 19 yard. This picture of the Margaret is from the files of Bob Beegle of Marcon who thinks it was supplied to Tom Mowbray by McAllister when they had her up for sale. The engine room and main deck house were all gutted. The pilothouse and stack scrapped. The new pilothouse w/Texas house and the new stack were fabricated right there in Tug & Barge. All the machinery, piping and electrical work where accomplished by our own people (I was one of them). The carpentry and joiner work was also done in-house by a superb gang of guys. This was nothing new to them though. They had converted tugs like the Roderick, Ellen F., Grace, John E., Eileen, Wm. H. and others before that and did quite a few after that, although not always steam conversions. Some were old direct drive diesels and some were old multiple engine diesel electrics.

All the U.S. Navy LST gear had become surplus and that's what most were getting. That's why we had right and left turning screws on different tugs. The LST's were twin screw and we used the entire port or starboard running gear for the conversions. The Margaret was repowered differently though with a surplus 16 cylinder 278 A of 1800 H.P. with a brand new reduction gear that was shifted hydraulically. Big thing at the time, also big horsepower. A new steel fuel tank was fabricated in place where the boilers used to be.

She had a lot of freeboard because when they took all the steam equipment and boilers out and put the new engine and reduction gear in it was nowhere near the same weight. They put a lot of Belgium blocks in for ballast but she was still high in the water and rolled a lot but didn't pitch much. We did a lot of mud work with her and were practically married to the Hess barge the 'Ethel H.' for a long while, on the coast to Wilmington, Delaware and running the same product back and forth between Raritan, Perth Amboy and the Woodbridge Hess plants.

When I first reported to the Margaret M. McAllister the engine room was in good shape as she hadn't been out of the yard too long and the chief, Arnold, was a stickler about cleanliness and new paint. As good as it looked, it looked a lot better after I was on it for a few months. The chief used to make me take the Belgium block ballast stones out of each bay, put them on newspaper and clean them, scrape and paint the bay they came out of and put them back. This was right after I had put a new coat of red shellac on the floor plates. Murder was not an option in those days, so I did as he said. The Margaret also had the typical McAllister fuel tank fabricated in place and about 16" off the bottom. Once we had a small leak in the hull under the tank and I was sent in with a hammer and tapered wooden plug (standard equipment in those days). I had a heck of a time squeezing in there. There were no Belgium blocks under the tank but it was full of muck and cold water because it was in the winter. There were a lot of stays and brackets in the way also. When I got to the leak I put the tip of the plug in the small hole and gave it a rap with the hammer. Yep, you guessed it, it went right through the hull and now water, ice cold water, was flying everywhere. It came up with such force (I think we drew about 13') that it hit the fuel tank bottom and the brackets and covered me with spray. To this day I don't really remember getting out, just the shock and fear. I had to come out backwards and I know I came out fast as all get out. Amazing what you can do when you have to. We called the office and got a diver in to stop it temporarily and went on dry dock for a doubler. Doublers were standard in those days and as everyone knows, they never lasted.

The Margaret was a big tug in those days and quiet and comfortable. The reason she was quiet was that the chief, Arnold, wouldn't let anyone run the main engine over 690 RPM even though the engine was rated at 750 RPM. She was comfortable though. She had a big half round galley table in the bow. We also installed a second door between the engine room and the companion way to the deckies quarters. That cut down on the engine noise quite a bit. Although a GM 16-278-A was fairly quiet on its own. And... she had a shaft generator, no noise from that. And when we did have to run the 6-71 generator engine in port when the batteries ran down it was at 1200 RPM, not the 1800/2100 RPM you have out there today. The engine room was large so the equipment was spread out in a very neat fashion.

There were two sets of quarters all the way aft for the black gang. Noisy, but to us it was white noise unless something was wrong, then we heard that immediately as we were right on top of the engine room. The quarters were relatively large and comfortable with lockers and a desk.

# Chapter 23 - Appendicitis

I was on the Margaret McAllister on the 6 to 12 watch and got sick before the watch was over and didn't want to eat at the midnight meal. I went to bed and was sick all night and started to throw up green. I knew what it was because I had appendicitis about two or three months before. I was so sick I could not get up. When I didn't get up for breakfast at 5:30 in the morning the chief came by on deck at 6 o'clock and yelled into my port light that was open with just the screen in place and said that I had to get up, it was time to go to work. I told the chief that I couldn't get up, I was too sick. He said never mind that Robert it's time for you to get up. Believe me, it was a bright warm day and I would normally be more than happy to jump out of my upper bunk. A little while later the deckhand Barney came into my room and said what's the matter Robert, the chief is really mad and I said "I'm very, very sick Barney, I think I have appendicitis". He could smell the vomit and said to wait and he will see if we can get you off the boat. He went up to the pilothouse and told Capt. Hans that I probably had appendicitis and had to get off the boat. All the while we had a head line out on a ship that was ready to sail and we were working slow ahead on the port bow. Capt. Hans said we couldn't leave the bow as the ship was getting ready to sail and the pilot would get mad. Barney said I think you better do something because Bob is really sick and we got to get him off the boat. Capt. Hans didn't want to do it because he was from the old school and didn't want to question authority, in this case the pilot. But Barney finally convinced him and he called the docking pilot on the radio and said they had to let the oiler off because he was really sick. The pilot said that it wasn't a problem and to do so right away. So Barney slacked off the line and the Capt. backed away and then came ahead and brought the bow against the dock. I got dressed with Barney's help and got off.

We were at the Brooklyn Army Terminal in Brooklyn, N.Y. and I had to go through security to get out of the terminal. When I showed my identification the guard wanted to know what was wrong, that I looked very sick and asked if I needed any help. I said no, I'll be okay. But after I left, I walked about a block and a half and fell into the gutter in pain. Everyone was walking around me and ignored me even though I was calling out and telling them that I was sick. A taxicab came by and the driver opened the passenger door and said "what's the matter fella you have a big night?" And I said "no, I'm sick as a dog, appendicitis, please take me over to the Marine Hospital in Staten Island and I'll pay you whatever you want". He got out of the cab and helped me in the back seat. He looked at me and said, no, no, you look too sick and I'm going to take you right up to the Norwegian hospital that is near here. He brought me to the hospital, went inside, got me a wheelchair, put me in it and brought me to the emergency room. He stayed with me until they interviewed me and took me away. I never paid him and I never thanked him. That always bothered me that I didn't know who he was and didn't thank him. Within an hour they operated on me as my appendix was ready to burst. The next day I woke up in the men's ward and had to pee so bad so I climbed over the bed railing that was in the raised position to go to the bathroom. The nurses came running and put me back in bed saying that I could not move because I had a spinal tap. I had no idea what a spinal tap was.

That same morning a pretty nurse's aide came to bathe me and as she was washing me and I was laying there naked I got an erection. Without a change in expression on her face she took the head of my penis in one hand and flicked the tip of it hard with the finger of her other hand and that was the end of that. She continued washing me like nothing ever happened, but I was embarrassed. I was in the hospital for three days before I was able to get to a telephone to call my parents to tell them where I was. They were very upset that no one had reported that I got off the boat sick and the chief and the captain both got in trouble with the main office and my father. After a couple of weeks off, I was back and all was well, almost as if nothing had ever happened.

# Chapter 24 - Birthday and Payback

The chief loved to tell stories about the old days and how great he was, how he was in the Norwegian Navy, how he was on Norwegian destroyers, how he was on Norwegian tank ships, how he was chief engineer on big yachts and how he was chief engineer on tugs of so many companies. He would tell us how many years he was in each position and how many years he was on the tugs with the different companies. One day I came into the galley in one of my wiseacre moods and said in front of everyone at the table "Happy Birthday Chief". He said, "but it's not my birthday Robert" and I said "oh yes but it is chief, I counted up all the time from your stories and I figure that you are a hundred and 20 years old today". Everyone started laughing but the chief was burning up. I might have thought it was a funny thing to do but I paid for it dearly. That afternoon he had me put up a ladder and climb into the inside of the smoke stack and paint the silencer (muffler) with aluminum paint while we were under way. I had to paint fast as the brush would stick to the silencer if I slowed down because it was so hot. The fumes from the paint going onto the hot silencer were terrible but I wasn't about to start complaining and give him the satisfaction. I got it done and never complained. One time I asked him about an electrical starting box for one of the large motors, he explained how it worked and like an asshole when I got home I tried to impress my father with my new found knowledge. He listened patiently and then said "What's the matter with you? Don't you have eyes of your own? Don't you have a brain of your own? Don't you have hands of your own? Now go back on board and open it up and use the diagram inside the starting box door and figure it out for yourself. It is nothing like what he told you!" I did and I learned that it probably was a good thing as I not only learned how a starting box worked but how to use your own common sense instead of listening to others.

Another time we had a Hess barge up to the town of Hudson on the Hudson River. After landing the barge, we went up to the city dock about 8:00 PM and tied up. After shutting down the engine and securing everything we all headed up the street to have a couple of beers leaving the cook on board to watch things. We had a nice time passing the bull and drinking beer when at 11:45 the chief turned to me and said "Robert, it is a quarter to 12. You have to go on watch at 12. I said you got to be kidding, the barge will not be ready until 8 or 9 tomorrow. No, no, you have to go on watch. The deckhand left with me and said to hell with him. We went to another joint to have few more beers, which we did but were afraid the chief and first assistant would get back ahead of us so we soon went back to the tug. We shouldn't have worried. They didn't get back until 3 or 4 in the morning drunk as skunks and arguing as loud as could be. Now normally, when we would get the jingle to start up, I would go below if I wasn't already there and start the pre-lube pump, start the hydraulic pumps for the reduction gear, open the sea suction, open the fuel valves, start the steering gear and open the start air valve, roll the engine over, close the test cocks and then the chief would come down and pull the air start valve and give the throttle a bump to start up. Then I would shut down the pre-lube pump and make sure all the water and oil pressures were up to snuff. I was never allowed to actually start the main engine myself. He would then nod to me and leave me in the engine room. Well, that morning when the captain rang the jingle to start up the chief and the first were dead to the world. The captain asked me if I could start the engine and I said "sure". I did and we got underway.

When the chief and the first finally got up nothing was said to me, not even thank you. So now the chief was having a late breakfast in the galley and the first assistant, Raul, came in through the companionway muttering to himself and looking around. He left through the portside watertight door and soon appeared at the starboard door still muttering. After a few minutes he came through the companionway door again and we asked him what was wrong. He didn't answer but kept muttering. We were worried but the chief seemed calm. We asked him what was going on and he said that when they were arguing in the galley last night, Raul was yelling so hard he blew his false teeth out of his mouth and that they were under the refrigerator. I got a paper towel and retrieved them just as Raul was coming into the galley again. I gave them to him and he muttered thank you and glared at the chief but didn't say anything.

A few weeks later the chief went on vacation to Norway. Raul was filling in for him so I was on his watch. One of the first things I did whenever I came on board was to go into the vee of the hull at the very aft end of the engine room and check the packing gland and tighten it if necessary as I had been instructed by the chief. You had to pull open a steel plate hatch and climb down into a very tight space. When I checked it the water was pouring in. Raul saw what I was doing and said, "no, no Robert, you can't touch that. Only the chief is allowed to adjust the packing gland". I said what are you nuts? The chief never climbs down here, he always has me do it. Besides, he won't be back for two weeks, we can't let it leak like it is. Raul was amazed but let me tighten the four nuts evenly while watching me the whole time. When I came up he said the chief told him he was the only one who adjusted gland. I just smiled.

Robert Mattsson

# Chapter 25 - Painting the Engine Room

One day the chief told me I had to start painting the engine room so when I came on watch I got the paint mixed. We always put a little bluing into the white paint before mixing. I set up a drop cloth and a brush and a roller and I went all the way aft to start painting. I figured I would start there and work my way forward. The chief came back and said to me, no, no, Robert you can never start painting in the back of the engine room. So I said well where do you want me to start chief, in the middle? He said come with me and I'll show you. Sure enough he took me right to the middle of the engine room and said start here. I said you got to be kidding, which way should I go forward or aft? Don't be smart he said, just start painting. This aggravated me but I got everything set up again and started to paint. Near the end of the watch I started to clean up and put away the drop cloths and close the paint cans and began to clean the paintbrushes in the fuel oil bucket we always kept at the front of the engine room under a fuel valve on the fuel tank bulkhead we used for various projects. The chief came over and said oh no Robert, we never clean paintbrushes in fuel oil. I said where the hell do you want me to clean them? I've been cleaning them in here for over a year. He looked dumbfounded and said to me, well don't stick them all the way in. Now I was really aggravated. I cleaned everything up and saw it was still 20 minutes to go before the end of the watch. So I went up and sat on the bench we had on the stern to cool off. The chief came up and put his arm around me and said what's wrong Robert are you sick? I said no I'm fine. So he said well what are you doing? You have been eff'in around all day and started sticking his fingers in my chest again and again. I pushed his hands away and stood up, but he kept doing it and I pushed his hands away again but he wouldn't stop yelling and sticking his fingers into my chest. So I pushed him away and he lost his balance and fell against the waist rail and almost went overboard. But I grabbed him and pulled him back. He went straight to the Captain and told him that I tried to push him overboard. They got to a telephone and called the port engineer, told their side of the story and he said they were to tell me I was fired. The next day when my father came home he asked, what the hell did you do? Now you lost a good job. I told him my side of the story and said I would try to get an oilers job with one of the other companies. He was annoyed but I think he felt I could be right. The next day he came home from work and said that the chief offered to take me back if I apologized. I told him I would not go back to work with him. He relayed this to Red Edmonds the Port Engineer. A few days later Mr. Edmonds called me and asked me to please go back that I didn't have to say I was sorry and the chief would take me back. He said they couldn't get any oiler to go to work for him. I thanked Mr. Edmonds but said I would try to get a job with Bronx Towing before going back to work with him. A few days later he called and said he had another opening for me but as my punishment I was going to have to work for the toughest chief engineer in the fleet, Bill Niedermayer on the Peter B. McAllister. That was bad enough but the Peter B was also a two weeks on and one week off boat whereas I had been working seven days on, three off, seven days, on four off. So I wasn't too happy and a little nervous when I got to the boat and met my new chief. I guess he was told that I was a wiseacre, bosses son who needed to be put in his place. So the first greeting was a little stiff. Well I just went about my business and started to work and clean up the engine room and learn the main engine and the controls because I hadn't been on a boat with a Superior main engine before. Before the week was out he was not only treating me as a regular guy but very, very well. I did my work and didn't complain and found what he wanted me to do was easy compared to what I had to do for Arnold on the Margaret McAllister. And that's how I ended up on the Peter B McAllister, one of the best jobs I have ever had. Bill Niedermayer taught me so many things and helped me study for my engineers license once he found out I was serious. I was having some trouble with the math and formulas so he taught me how to do it the European way which made me understand the way I was taught a lot better and then it all came together.

# Chapter 26 - Peter B. McAllister

Peter B. McAllister - 80.2' x 22.6' x 9.9'; 142 gt, 95 nt. 8 cylinder Superior Direct Drive Diesel, 14.5 x 20, 750-bhp.

There were eight men as crew on a canaler when the oiler was on. The tugs were small because that was what was needed in the New York State Barge Canal System. Small in length to fit in a lock along with the oil barge you were pushing and small in height to fit under all the fixed bridges. On most canal tugs you couldn't stand up straight in the galley unless you were 5' 8". The oil burning stove was so hot in the summer you were soaking wet by the time you were finished eating and went outside to the cool evening air of 95 degrees. The stove/oven was a WebbPerfection oil stove, made of steel with a cast iron top. The fire box was lined with fire brick and asbestos cement. At the bottom was a well about 2 inches wide and 6 to 8 inches long. A manual fuel oil carburetor fed diesel oil into the well and you could adjust the carburetor to a lower burning rate or a higher burning rate to somewhat control the temperature. With the different fuel rates you had to adjust the 110 Volt DC blower. As the motor turned at a more or less constant speed (it would fluctuate with the

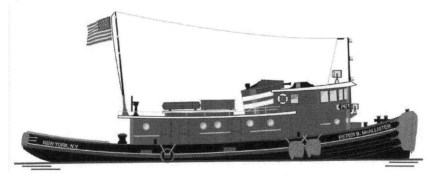

voltage being put out from the shaft generator) you had to adjust the blower air flap. Everyone in the crew thought they were an expert at this and would keep adjusting the carburetor or air damper when no one was looking resulting in a very hot flame or a very smoky one. The rule was, no one touched these controls except the cook and the oiler but nobody seemed to care. Sometimes the cook top would get so hot it would glow red. Soot and a hard crust would form from the impurities in the fuel and it was the oilers job to clean it out at least once a week on the 12 to 6 AM watch. My hands were ingrained with black soot for two days even though I washed them in fuel oil and lye soap. The carburetor also had to be cleaned and the little DC motor had to have the commutators sanded and cleaned constantly and the brushes changed occasionally. The motors had a habit of burning out because of the high voltage swings so we always tried to keep two spares on board. However they were hard to come by and the ones we got were not new, but rebuilt. Sometimes they only lasted a couple of days. Once or twice a year we had to clean the exhaust flue as the soot would build up and we would get a smoke build-up in the galley. I have to hand it to the cooks though, they could boil, fry and bake on that thing better than most could on a gas oven. For steaks they would turn the heat up high, throw a slab of butter down and the steak on top of that and it would immediately sizzle with a big cloud of smoke and cook real fast. They were delicious and great for your cholesterol, although we didn't know anything about cholesterol then. A coffee pot ( a percolator) was always going on the stove top. The coffee was real thick and if you made it any other way there was hell to pay. The coffee basket was always filled to the very top. The cooks would make their own hot cross buns, pies and cakes as well as roasts in that oven and they were always delicious. I slept in an upper bunk that when you went to turn over you hit your shoulder on the overhead. There was one shower on board with no hot water after the first burst of steam. Cockroaches so common you didn't notice them anymore. No insulation of any kind, wall or sound. Only the asbestos on the exhaust. And there was plenty of that.

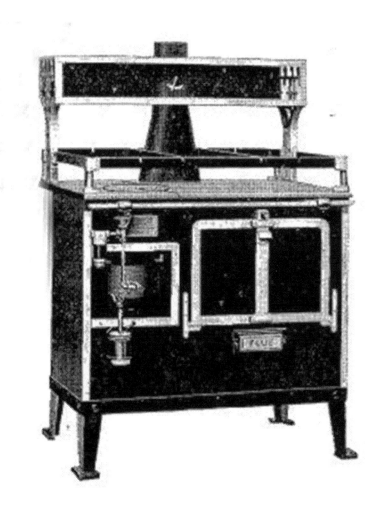

No TV, no radio, no automatic coffee maker and a newspaper every couple of days if you were lucky. Paperback books you traded other boats for when we would meet up. We washed our clothes on the hawser rack over the steering quadrant with a scrubbing brush and brown soap. Then tied them with rope and put them in the propeller wake for the rinse. Then we hung them in the engine room or up on the boat deck rails to dry, stiff as a board, but clean. However, the crew were all great guys, we went swimming naked, played pinochle, poker, chess, went "up street", steered into weird places, met weird people, hung out in the pilot house in the dark on the 12 to 6 and talked about family, hopes and dreams or what you were going to do on your time off. Same when we were waiting for a lock and met in the galley for coffee and a smoke. It was also great to get together and change crew with these friends.

We did get a radio after a while. The chief's wife bought him a battery operated portable radio about the size of a small piece of luggage for his birthday. They were a big deal at the time. Although we would listen to music, what we really wanted was to be able to get the weather report when we were on the Great Lakes as the weather was very unpredictable and came on you fast. Well, we gathered on the railing in the evening on our next trip on Lake Erie and got the radio going. It was fairly hard to find a station, you had to carefully tune it while rotating it at the same time but when we did get one we all listened to hear the weather. After 5 or 6 minutes of music and commercials, the announcer would come on and identify the station. It would be from Texas! We fiddled around until we got another station and after waiting the announcer would get on and identify the station as coming from Kentucky. Well this went on for a few more times and we could not pull in a local station. The chief got so mad he said he was going to tell his wife to return it and get one that could receive broadcasts from the Great Lakes region. I told him that all radios were the same and there had to be some other problem. The next night the weather was different and the radio was bringing in all the local stations. There was some kind of temperature inversion in the atmosphere that was blocking the local signals and allowing the distant ones to bounce off the weather layer and get picked up by our little radio. Now the chief was happy with his new radio.

# Chapter 27 - The Firing Range

"Good morning Carl" I said pleasantly to the deckhand as he sat down to breakfast.

"Ya", he answered grumpily.

"What do you want this morning?" asked Cookie. "Vy, do ya have something different today? He asked sarcastically. Oh boy, I thought to myself, it's going to be one of those days. Usually when we got near the end of our two-week tour on the canal tug 'Peter B. McAllister' I was the one who got grumpy and edgy. I wanted to be home with my beautiful wife and the crew knew this and would tease me until I blew my stack or I got off the boat. And I could usually get off the boat first if we were near land, another tug or a bridge I could jump to because as the oiler I didn't have to shake hands with my relief like the rest of the crew. As soon as the chief said I could go, I would begin scheming on how I was going to accomplish this.

Barney settled for eggs, bacon, sausage, potatoes and toast while I ate my oatmeal with fresh farm cream we had picked up the day before in Toledo. I had been diagnosed with a stomach ulcer and believe it or not, at that time the doctor recommended cream to sooth the stomach and the cook went out of his way to get me fresh cream. Carl was mumbling about not having fish for breakfast when Captain Vic came stumbling and grumbling in. The captain wasn't grumpy because tomorrow was crew change. He was grumpy because he was Captain Vic and he was always grumpy. Instead of talking to the two grumpy Norwegians I kept eating and looking down at the brown linoleum tabletop covered for the most part with a red and white-checkered tablecloth. The table and the refrigerator underneath it were built into the bulkhead between the galley and the foc's'le. It was a work of art but it was the only boat I had been on up to then that had brown linoleum for the table top instead of green.

This was real canvas backed linoleum, about 3/16" thick, not the stuff you put on your floors today. Cookie scrubbed it every day and then wiped it with cooking oil to make it shine. I was wondering who got to pick the color when the port door opened and the chief engineer, Bill (his real name was Norbert) came in with his normal cheerful demeanor and fresh scrubbed looks. A nice looking man, he always kept himself and his clothes immaculate. He was a very orderly and talented engineer. From Germany, he would sit and tell me stories about inflation in the old country when he was a youngster that would amaze me. He also had many stories about the yachts he worked on in the old days. The stories weren't told though until my work was finished and he had me go over my studies. I was studying for my engineer's license and I just knew that if I didn't put everything I had into it and failed when I sat before the Coast Guard examiner he was going to take it personally. I was studying on my time off at the Seaman's Church Institute in Manhattan but was having trouble with the square root that was needed for all the horse power formulas. I also had a lot of trouble with algebra and geometry that I failed to pay attention to in Curtis High School. Bill taught me the European way which clicked with me and made me understand the American way. He was a great teacher.

That reminds me of the time I was sitting for my engineers license at the Customs House building in lower Manhattan. We always wore suits at the time and I had a brown wool suit on one day. We always went back to our teacher at the Seaman's Institute at lunch time to tell them what questions we were asked and go over what we thought was coming next (we were never right). The Seaman's Institute was about 8 blocks from the Custom House and it was raining pretty hard. By the time I got back to the exam room from the Seaman's Institute I was soaking wet and my wool suit smelt terrible. It distracted me for a while and I thought everybody noticed but I finally got caught up in the questions and forgot about it.

Bill helped the cook get his meal on the table because it was 0545 already and then poured his own coffee. There wasn't much talk at the table, the cook was babbling to the captain about grub money (again) and the captain just grunted back. We always thought the captain and the cook were pocketing some of the grub money and on some boats it was a real problem. Something was up with Carl the deckhand but I couldn't tell what it was and I had my own thoughts anyway. If we couldn't make it to Tonawanda, N.Y., the Western entrance to the Erie Barge Canal by tomorrow afternoon then we would have to change crew at Syracuse a day or more later. This would not only mean we would get home a day later but would lose a day of time off. It was relatively calm on Lake Erie today and we were in pushing gear with the barge in ballast so we should make it across the lake in 25 to 28 hours. A few days ago on the way to Toledo, heading west it started out smooth but the weather changed so quick it caught us off guard and all hands were needed to get the pushing gear and steamboat ratchets in and the towing bridles and hawser out. We were all soaking wet and tired but felt like we beat the weather and saved the day. Then we were in for a rough 12 hours of towing on the hawser. I got real sick and was kneeling on the deck and holding onto the fender bar under the railing and wanted to die as I was heaving. The waves would come over the rail and engulf me. I had to hold on for dear life as it would lift or float me up. An hour later I was in the galley eating, trying to make up for what I threw up into Lake Erie. Now I was hoping the weather would hold so we could make good time across the lake. I would try to get off at Tonawanda but the captain and chief would worry about me putting in for expenses from a different port then the rest of the crew if they changed crew in Syracuse. I would tell them that this was the 60's and it didn't matter to the office but they were from the old school and I was not going to change the way they thought.

    Bill asked me what my project for the day was going to be and I answered that I was going to do general cleaning and get ready for crew change. Actually I was going to try to do as little as possible because after two weeks I was getting tired of it. I still had to do the brass tonight before we changed crew, if we changed crew, so maybe I would sneak in a little of that in the lower engine room this morning. There was a lot of brass on all these older tugs and I was dopey enough to find more. I would scrape and sand the bonnets on our larger valves so I could shine them and scrape the paint off copper lines and tubing so I could polish them also. However the engine room looked great and the chief was proud so it made me feel good and proud also.

The captain got up and went to relieve the mate without picking up his dishes. He never did, after all, he was the "Captain". Carl got up and put his dishes in the sink and went below to the foc's'le sleeping quarters to get his gear and pipe and tobacco so he wouldn't bother his colleague while he was off watch and in the rack. The chief was finishing up when I put my dishes in the sink, poured myself more coffee and sat down again. I should have went to the engine room, made my rounds and relieved the first assistant so the chief could relax but I was afraid the 'First' had some of his work that he wanted to pawn off on me. He could do this when the chief wasn't around because technically he was my boss too. Of course, on a small tug everyone is the oiler's "boss". Finally Bill cleared his spot, poured more coffee to take with him and thanked the cook. I noticed the steering shaft running along the overhead of the galley moving one way and then the other. It had been almost motionless the whole time we ate breakfast because we were steering a course on Lake Erie from Toledo to Buffalo and there was no reason to be turning the rudder to any great degree. Captain Vic was a nervous, antsy type of guy when he wasn't drinking and he never drank on board. There was no alcohol allowed on the tug but "up the street" was a different story and it looked like he was "up the street" last night. When he was on watch, especially on open water he would walk from the port side of the low silhouette pilothouse to the starboard side and take a spoke of the wheel in his hand and bring it with him as he went. Then he would do the same on the way back. Our wake looked like a snakes path.

    Watching the steering shaft move reminded me that I had to clean the commutator and blow out the carbon dust on the Direct Current steering gear motor. I also had to grease the steering gear and slush the steering chains before I got off so now was a good time to do it. I hurried out of the galley and into the upper engine room where the chief and the first assistant were talking and quickly told Bill what I was about to do. He nodded appreciatively as the first assistant tried to tell me something but I quickly turned and using the handrails only, slid down the ladder to the lower engine room. I liked it in the lower engine room, the big, 750 horsepower (we called it 880 HP), eight cylinder Superior Diesel engine was thumping away at 270 RPM in tune with the valve gear clicking and clacking, the 5 foot diameter flywheel making a whooshing kind of noise and the belts driving the main air compressor from the intermediate shaft pulley slapping away. All the sounds sort of blended together but if one of the sounds stopped or changed in pitch or volume a good engineer would know immediately that something was wrong or had changed and would investigate.

I finished the steering gear maintenance in just over an hour. Everything went relatively smooth, partly because Captain Vic kept moving the rudder and that made it easier to slush the chains. I washed up in the tiny sink on the starboard side and climbed the ladder to the upper engine room. Bill was sitting on the settee in front of the engine operating controls reading the paper. I got on top of the engine, standing on the heads and oiled the valve stems with the fuel/lube /Marvel Mystery oil mixture and the rocker bearings and rollers with lube oil. When I was done I sat on the settee next to Bill and we talked about the end of the canal season. This was when the locks would freeze, the levels would be low and frozen and the tug would go into the shipyard for overhaul. I wasn't worried about being laid off because even if the company didn't keep the whole crew on during the overhaul they always kept the chief and the oiler. The chief they kept for his knowledge and the oiler was kept to do the dirty work.

    Carl had been walking back and forth along the deck and I finally realized he was trying to get my eye. He held his fingers up to his mouth and tilted his head back indicating I should join him for coffee. Cookie was in the rack as was the mate, assistant engineer and deckhand from the opposite watch.

Barney had a chart out on the table. "What's up Carl? What are you doing with a chart down here?" It was unusual to take the charts out of the pilothouse, especially during daylight. "Ya, you vant to get off in Tonawanda don'cha". "Yeah, but why the chart and how come you're so anxious, you never care when you get off?" "Vell" said Carl, "my daughter is in a play or something at school the day after tomorrow and my vife vants me there". "Well that's great but what are you worried about? We'll make it, we will just be a little late". Carl then told me that captain Vic was going to steer North to avoid a large military firing range instead of going straight through because the Notice to Mariners indicated they would start at 0900 today. If we lost a couple or three hours and had to slow at all for weather then when we called in tonight the dispatchers would say 1800 or 1900 hours tomorrow was too late to change crew and would reschedule us for the next day at Syracuse.

Neither one of us wanted that to happen. "Well, what can we do?" I asked. "Vell Bobby boy (when he pronounced my nickname it sounded more like Boppy then Bobby) I have a plan".

The plan was to try and get Vic out of the pilothouse or distracted with the log book or charts or anything that would keep him occupied while Carl steered a straight course and I jacked the engine RPMs up a little to make better speed. First though, we would have to convince Vic that we could cover the distance and be clear of the firing range before 0900. Then we set up the rest of our plan.

"Hey Bill, do you want to play pinochle?" I asked. "In the morning?" he asked. "Well, yeah, I figure we are on a long run, Carl can steer and I'll ask Vic if he wants to play". When I reached the pilothouse Carl was already trying to convince Vic that we could cover the distance by 0900. Captain Vic wasn't buying it though, he was afraid we would get in trouble if we didn't clear the area on time. I told him we would certainly make it and if it got close and it didn't look good, we could speed up the engine and make it for sure. Which was quite big of me because I did not know how far we had to go or what speed we were making at the time. I also said we didn't know for sure if they were even going to be firing today. Carl piped up with the point that if we were close to the end of the restricted area that would be okay too because they probably only fired live shells in the middle of the area. That seemed to make sense to Vic and to me, so while he was still nodding in agreement I told him that the chief wanted to play pinochle, and asked if he was in. He brightened right up and said "Ya sure. In the morning?"

I got the worn out pinochle cards from the galley pantry and put the coffee on, filling the basket to the top so it would be the way they liked it, strong and bitter, Bill made the rounds in the engine room to make sure everything was running well and Vic filled out his log and set the course for Carl to steer.

The first three hands we all passed on and on the forth Bill bid 340. Bill made his bid and Vic blamed it on me. This was not a good start, I didn't need Vic to get mad and storm off to the pilothouse. We passed again and then Vic won the bid with a measly 290 but it was in spades and he covered the bid in his meld so he didn't have to play it out and we had to pay him double, which made him very happy. While Vic was dealing I ran off to the engine room and pushed the throttle up one notch moving the injector wedges in ever so slightly and came back to the galley. We were looking at our new hands when Bill said to me "Did you raise the RPMs?" Jeez, I thought, it was only one notch, how the heck did he notice that? "Yeah, well the exhaust temperatures looked a little low, I guess the headwind died down," I said. "Ve didn't have a headwind this morning" murmured Vic as he set up his cards. Bill didn't say any more and I just looked at my cards. The steering shaft over our heads was hardly moving so Carl was holding up his end but I needed to get the engine speed up one more notch to make a difference. We played for about another 10 minutes and so far I hadn't won a hand because all I could think about was getting the engine speed up one more notch. Cookie came into the galley and asked to sit in. This was great because with four playing everyone took a turn sitting out. When you sat out you paid or collected but didn't have a hand.

When it was my turn to sit out I went to the engine room and very, very slowly pushed the throttle up one notch. The engine sounded a lot louder and faster to me. All the sounds seemed to increase in volume and frequency, the vibrations felt worse also and I expected the chief to come running into the engine room any second. He didn't, but when I got back to the galley he gave me a funny look. He must know what's going on I said to myself. He made rounds at 0800 and came back to the galley without saying anything and I didn't hear or feel the engine speed being lowered. At 0830 I had to oil the top of the engine and wipe up. The engine was running well and at the RPM I last set it at. Instead of moving the throttle up another notch, I turned the thumbscrew on each injector rocker down a little which would increase the fuel without pushing the fuel wedge in any more, sort of fine tuning and getting a couple of more RPM without the speed jumping up in a larger increment where the chief would notice. I went up to the bow and through the open pilothouse window asked Carl how he was doing. He indicated everything was fine and smiled with his pipe in his teeth. He looked pleased with himself and very relaxed. Back in the galley by 0845 and the cook and the captain were yelling at each other and Bill was getting more coffee. Bill was out and I was in, the cook had won so he was dealing. We all seemed to get a good hand so there was a lot of cautious bidding that was taking a long time when at 0900 on the button Carl blew the whistle, blew down the voice tube and started to shout out the window. We all jumped up and ran out to see what the hell was going on. Even the deckhand and mate that were off watch came running out in their underwear to see what was happening. "What is it", they yelled, fire? Collision? Are we sinking? Carl said "Vic, you better get up here, the Army is on the radio screaming at you for being in this zone". Vic went pale and started to stutter, Carl said he wasn't going to answer the radio, the chief wanted to know what was wrong and the mate said he hoped we hadn't tried to go through the firing zone! Bill shot me a look that said 'now I know what you were up to'. I was red in the face, Carl was scared to death and Captain Vic was in shock. Vic made his way to the pilothouse and Bill told me to go with him and help out. Vic answered the frantic radio call with a trembling voice and a heavy accent. The officer on the other end wanted to know what we doing there, why we didn't know this was a prohibited zone, that we had almost been fired on, what was the name of the unit, where were we from, what company did we belong to, what was the captains name, what was his USCG license number, what was the official number of the boat, how many crew on board, how could we be so stupid. Well, Captain Vic was just about in tears and couldn't talk. To be questioned and yelled at by someone in authority, especially the federal government was incomprehensible to anyone on board. They called twice more before Vic shakily picked up the microphone and began to answer in Norwegian. Carl and I both began to yell at him and this just made things worse. I took the mike and said the captain was going to get his license number and the other information they wanted, that this would take about 10 minutes and what did they want us to do in the meantime? The guy on the other end seemed to calm down a little and asked how long we would be before we were out of the zone, I looked at Barney and he said "half hour", "Are you sure Carl, I don't want these people coming after us!". "Na, ve vill make it, you'll see". So I told him half an hour and in fact we were out of the zone in just over

20 minutes. When Vic had collected his composure and papers, we read them off to the officer on the other end of the VHF radio and he said he would be contacting our office and that made all of us sick to our stomachs. When I got back to the engine room Bill was not at all talkative and I noticed the engine speed was back down to normal full.

That watch and our next were not very happy and there was very little chatter. I think that if the captain wasn't so embarrassed by his lack of composure he would have fired Carl on the spot. We finally made it to Tonawanda and changed crew. Carl made his daughters play which made his wife and daughter happy and when we came back a week later all was forgiven except for a little deserved hazing for Carl and I. We never heard anymore from the firing range and we never sailed through that section again.

# Chapter 28 - NYS Barge Canal Things

We had a runner who was like an area supervisor for McAllister based in Rensselaer, NY. His name was Paul and he was called the 'Spider'. We were tied up once on a wall before a bridge on the Erie Canal for high water when he came with his rope and ruler, had us measure the distance from the water to the underside of the bridge. Then we stuck the pipe pole out and measured from the top of the stack on the Peter B. to the water. This was our highest point. We were too high. So he got us plywood, we cut it to fit in front of the scuppers in the waist that allow water to run off the deck in heavy weather . We held it in place with wooden wedges. Stuffed rags in the openings and pumped water on deck with our bilge/fire pump and at the same time filled the bilges to the floor plates. Then we kept the fire pump on and opened the hydrants on deck to flood it. All the time we were measuring. When we got close, but still too high, the 'Spider' told us to back down and then come up river. When we reached the bridge I was to give all the speed we had so we would suck down in the canal and clear the remaining inches. We were pushing a loaded Gulf barge so we weren't going to go any too fast. Just before the bridge I got another jingle and pushed the Superior main engine to the limit so we would suck down in the water. Well, we gave it our all and still hit one of the I beams right smack in the middle of our stack. That crease in the stack fairing was there for many years. We didn't damage the bridge and had no serious damage to the tug except for the crease and the captain's nerves. We kept going as the 'Spider' paid off the lock tenders with beer and/or ice cream so we could continue and they would maneuver the dam gates for us at the right time. Paul was the local man on the spot. He had relatives in the main office and the shipyard. He was not mechanically inclined but had other attributes. He could get you anything if you could convince him it was needed for the tug to operate. He could deliver ice cream and/or beer to a lock and the dam gates would magically open or close to allow the level to change so we could get under a bridge or over the bottom.

He would always bring me his Tiffany lamps that he collected for me to repair. I was very good at soldering so he always had a lamp shade for me to repair. I didn't mind though, as a matter of fact, I enjoyed it. He was also good at talking to the local authorities when a crew member got in trouble in Rensselaer or Albany.

To save money for McAllister and to get to some spots in the canal system that didn't have ready transportation he would pick us up at the Albany train station and drive us the rest of the way and bring the other crew back. He had a Chevrolet station wagon and he always had two or three 5 gallon cans of gasoline siphoned from the bottoms of the Gulf Oil barges after they pumped out, in the back of the station wagon. He would drive the small, local, two lane roads at over 90 mph in the fog aimed right down the white line in the middle of the road with us smoking and the gas sloshing in the back of the station wagon. A bomb waiting to happen that never did. McAllister had a lot of equipment running up that way and he kept everyone one on their toes and did the communicating with the main office which was not easy for the crew in those days as radios couldn't make the distance and pay telephones were far and few between. He was always on the go during the season and disappeared in the winter only to reappear again the next season.

We had a deck hand who was somewhat of a naturalist and liked to sleep outside in the afternoons. There was a problem though, he liked to sleep naked to get the sun and stay cool. He removed all the paint from our paint locker on the upper deck. The locker was a wooden box about 6 foot long and 2 1/2 feet wide with a hinged top. He would place a couple of blankets in the box with a pillow and lay down naked thinking no one could see him. Well, he got away with it for a long time but one day we were going under one of the low bridges and there were some tourists on the bridge checking out the wonders of the canal. They looked down and saw wonders they were not expecting, him not 10 feet below from where they were standing. They called the police and at the next lock they came aboard and woke him up. We thought it was funny and so did the police, he just got a warning and we got underway again.

    We had one shower, one head in the same little space for 8 men. So, urinating over the side at that time was not unusual. The cook in his high white cook's hat and white apron was going over the side as we rounded a bend in the canal and he was looking down, aiming and not up at his surroundings. Well, there was a party going on in someone's backyard at this spot. The party goers saw him and started screaming at him as he tried his best to stop and put it back in. They called the State Police and a Trooper met us at the next lock and after the cooks explanation and the captain saying it wouldn't happen again, the Trooper gave us a warning.

    We worked 2 weeks on and 1 week off in the canal at that time. The watches were 6 hours on and 6 hours off. You ate on your off watch. If you were on the 12 to 6 watch, you ate at 11:30 and after 6 when you were relieved. At midnight you made your own meal. Left over's, bacon and eggs, sardine and onion sandwiches, cereal or peanut butter and jelly. And coffee, always coffee. There was always plenty of food. The cooks were great. Roasts, steaks, chops, potatoes, fresh vegetables, oatmeal, eggs, fried potatoes, bacon, you name it we got it. They baked their own cakes and pies and rice pudding, bread pudding and some fish stuff I wouldn't eat. Off watch you took a shower, shaved or washed up, washed your clothes, wrote a letter or postcard home, cleaned your room, read a book, studied for your license, played pinochle, poker or gin rummy and occasionally chess.

    Sleeping during the day in the summer was difficult because it was so hot and there was no air conditioning on the tugs at that time. My bunk was the upper and I couldn't turn over without hitting my shoulder on the pressed board used for the overhead. If you put your hand on the overhead during a sunny summer day it was hot to the touch. That heat transferred to your body as you tried to sleep.

The canal was very dark at night and we used search lights mounted on the barge forward of mid ships and operated them by small clothes line type rope and pulleys that went all the way back to the tug pilot house. The captain and deck hand would each take a side to operate the lines as needed. This way they could see the canal banks and keep going at night. They also provided warning to us of oncoming traffic as well as letting them know we were approaching.

I was just married and would want to get home as soon as possible when my time off was coming up. A few times I stood on top of the smoke stack as we approached a bridge and as we went under I grabbed onto the bridge works and climbed onto the bridge. Then I would hitchhike to a bus terminal. One time I got off in Whitehall, and asked where the Greyhound bus stop was. I was told where it stopped and was standing there for about an hour when a police car approached and the officer asked me what I was doing here. When I told him, he said the bus didn't come until 10:00 AM the next morning. So I hitch hiked to somewhere that I could get to a train station. In those days you could always get a ride by sticking out your thumb.

The Gulf Oil barges we pushed into the canal would take 10 to 12 hours to pump the product off. This included sounding the tanks when we arrived and again after declaring the tanks empty. During this period we would do maintenance. The deck crew would chip, scrape and paint and the engine crew would do machinery maintenance. This could be as simple as changing out packing on the pumps, or a little more time consuming like changing out valve cages on the main engine. The cages and valves were rebuilt and lapped in when we were underway to get ready for the next chance when we shut down for a period of time. Sometimes we would change a head or re-ring a piston if we thought it was needed and we had the time. The deckhands would usually help on that type of job. After we were finished with the maintenance we would go as a group to a local bar and have a few beers. We always had at least two men stay aboard.

One time as we were coming into Sylvan Beach on Oneida Lake the crew was on deck trying to figure out a way to get the mate, Frank B. up on time. He was always hard to wake up and was constantly late for his watch. They were all huddled by the galley door, not far from his bunk room. His watertight door was open but had a screen door on it. They decided to roll up some newspaper, light it on fire, throw it into his room and yell "fire!". Well, he overheard them as he had been laying awake because of the heat and he knew where we were also. At Sylvan Beach there are a lot of marinas and we were on a slow bell. So, as soon as they threw the lit paper in and yelled fire, he came flying out the door and dove overboard. The captain rang for full astern, blew the alarm on our horn (probably woke up everybody in Sylvan Beach) and played our searchlight over the area. No Frank. We called and yelled but no Frank. Finally he popped up and swam over with a smirk on his face. He told us later that he had overheard us and when we looked for him with the searchlight, he swam underwater long enough to give us a scare. He swam to the stern quarter and pulled himself up on the pushing wires to the deck, smiling all the time.

# Chapter 29 - Cockroaches

I left the engine room and came into the galley of the tug Peter B. McAllister through the portside Dutch door and saw that the cook was peeling potatoes over on the starboard side of the galley table. "Hi Cookie" I said as I went to get my coffee from the big aluminum percolator on top of the oil burning stove. "Harrumph" he answered back. When I brought my coffee over to the table to put my sugar and milk in I saw he was pushing something away with the back of his right hand, the one he had the potato peeler in. I looked closer and realized it was a cockroach. "Whoa", I said, what are you doing? What the heck's a matter with you, why don't you kill it? Are you kidding, he answered, if I kill every cockroach that comes to the table it will soon be so disgusting you guys will be complaining about their bodies all over the table. When I kill them they keep on coming. I said that's awful but he countered with, "That's the way it is". With that he pushed another one back. And it was true, after awhile we all got used to seeing cockroaches everywhere. At first we would kill them on the red and white checkered tablecloth but it made a mess. Eventually we just watched them. It was so bad and we got so used to them and we would actually wait until a cockroach would crawl across and over the potatoes or vegetables in the serving dishes and would wait until they moved off before grabbing your portion. We had bought insecticides at the hardware stores and got what we could from the company but nothing seemed to halt their advance in any way at all. After a while no one said anything, unless we got a new crew member on board. We got so used to it we didn't even think about it anymore.

I had just gotten married and the Peter B. was going to be tied up for the New Year's holiday. I was selected as the watchman for her and ten or twelve other tugs that were also going to be laid up at Pier 13 North River in Manhattan for the holiday. Naturally I wanted to be with my wife, Gail, as we were just married the previous August and I wanted to spend the holiday with her. I called and asked if she would come and stay overnight on the tug with me. She was staying with her parents while I was away and they didn't want her to go. They didn't know anything about tugs or Pier 13 and didn't like the idea. I talked her into it anyway. She and her family weren't too happy but she said yes to please me.

I checked the bilges and batteries of all the boats in my care and then drove quickly over to Staten Island to pick her up and bring her back to Manhattan. I worried that someone would check up on me and find me gone or a boat would start to leak and sink. I needn't have worried, no one ever checked on me and the closest I ever came to a serious problem was a year or so earlier when the wooden tug Teresa McAllister that was part of the fleet I was watchman for was leaking so bad through her planking and exacerbated by a severely leaking stern gland that when I went to check on her the water was above her floor plates. I found this out as I descended the steep engine room ladder in the dark and was suddenly standing in 8 to 10 inches of sea water. To compound the matter, the ships batteries were dead and the 2-71 diesel engine that ran the 20KW generator also had a dead battery. Luckily for me (and the company) the Teresa had a single cylinder 71 series generator that was hand cranked. This engine was normally hard to crank and start but I guess because I was scared to death and my adrenaline was up, I cranked that sucker up and got her running right away. Just in time too, as the water was reaching the electric motor of the bilge pump. Once I got the power to the switchboard and started the bilge pump and got some lights on, I went to the upper engine room, found the gasoline emergency pump, connected the hose and got that going also. Once the water level went down I discovered the leaking packing gland, tightened it up and all was well.

So anyway, I picked Gail up and raced back to Manhattan. We had to park under the Westside Highway structure and make our way out on the pitch black Pier 13 with only my flashlight to guide the way. She didn't like this at all. The pier had been abandoned for quite awhile for regular use and was in disrepair with holes in the deck and holes in the overhead. At the end of the pier we had to climb down a wooden ladder. Gail wasn't happy but she closed her eyes and made it to the deck of the tug that was against the pier as the tug and the ladder surged up and down. We had three more tugs to climb over until we got to the Peter B.

I had everything planned. We would stay in my room that I had scrubbed and cleaned, changed the bed linens and shined the stainless steel sink. Then just before midnight we would go up into the pilothouse and get set to blow the air horn to help celebrate the coming of 1962. Then we would come back to my room and celebrate as husband and wife.

So we got settled and sat for awhile in my room and then I said, "Okay let's go, let's go and blow the whistle it's almost midnight." All the rooms had outside doors so we went out and walked up the dark deck. I said to myself "I should have turned the deck lights on". Normally I kept them off to conserve battery power but to make her more comfortable I should have turned them on. To get to the pilothouse we were going to go through the galley, though the companionway, through the foc's'le access and then up to the pilothouse. I opened the steel weather tight Dutch door and told her to step over the high sill as I turned the galley lights on. Well, you wouldn't believe the sight. To this day I get the willies, but Gail absolutely shrunk down and screamed at the same time. The floor and table was a black mass of moving cockroaches. They were so thick you could barely make out the red deck paint. I thought she was going to faint. My god it was awful. They were scrambling to get back behind the walls after the light came on. Gail backed out the door so fast I had to grab her to keep from going overboard because the galley light had temporary blinded her and she didn't know where she was. She was screaming and crying but when I looked back into the galley they were almost all gone. She didn't care, she wanted to go home. She was gagging and still whimpering. She said she was not going back in my room, she didn't want to stay. I said "It's alright, it's alright". I told her they were not in the pilothouse or the rooms because there was no food there. I finally convinced her to come back in the galley and I quickly went up to the pilothouse and turned the lights on before she came up just in case.

We went up to the pilothouse and as it turned midnight we blew the horn and kissed. We went back through the galley to my room but the lights were still on so there was no sign of the cockroaches. She was itchy and squirmy all night long though and this put a large damper on my amorous plans. I drove her to her parent's home first thing in the morning, she didn't want to stay for breakfast. I don't know why.

On January $2^{nd}$ when we came out to go to work I told the crew what had happened. They couldn't believe there were that many. I told them to turn the lights out at night and see what happens. The galley lights were normally never turned off when we were operating so we had never witnessed this before. Well they tried it and confirmed that what I had said, I saw.

We were scheduled to go into the shipyard in February for our annual overhaul and reported the problem to our Port Captain and Port Engineer.

Well, we went into the shipyard and began the overhaul. The third day the exterminator came and set himself up with a backpack pump sprayer and began spraying a chemical in the forepeak and worked his way aft. I don't know what kind of magic potion he had in there but the cockroaches were coming out of every crack and opening in the walls and the overheads. You could almost hear them screaming. Then they began falling out of the cracks and crevices between the galley and the engine room. They were falling on the engine, in the cylinders we had apart and the on mechanics heads and in their collars, dead, half dead and alive. The guys were wriggling and screaming and took off to the safety of the dock. We closed the boat up and no one was going to go back that day, and some said forever. The next day when we opened the doors it was unbelievable. They were covering the galley floor 2" deep and covered the floor plates in the engine room. We use brooms and shovels to pick them up and throw them over the side. It was truly disgusting. No one could believe it, they never saw that many cockroaches at one time in one place. To this day I don't know what chemical the exterminator used but I was on the Peter B. for another year and a half and I never saw a cockroach again!

# Chapter 30 - Shifting At Brooklyn Piers

Jingle... The cowbell at the control stand rang once. "Aw nut's" I said out loud. We were hanging on at Red Hook, Brooklyn waiting for a job and it was a good time for me as the assistant engineer to get some maintenance done on the tug's main engine bilge pump. The tugboat had a direct drive Superior main engine and when we weren't underway the engine was stopped. All the electrical was direct current and as we hadn't been shutdown long we were still on battery power. This made for a very quiet and peaceful atmosphere in which to get the job done that I wanted to do. On the front of the main engine was a twin piston double acting pump that ran off the main engine camshaft anytime the engine was running. This arrangement kept the bilge dry. The leather disk valves needed cleaning and the shaft packing had to be changed so the pump could draw the bilge water up the five feet without losing its suction and at the same time water would not leak into the pump area of the engine block and then make its way into the crankcase.

I was hurrying to get it back together again when my buddy, Carl the deckhand yelled down to me "get 'er going Row'bert ve have to do some shifting ya know". "All right, all right, Carl but I need 5 minutes to get this back together again ". "Okay" said Carl "but you better get the 'Hurdy Gurdy' going too. Ve have to hurry up with the shifting to clear the pier and then help the Ellen F. in vith a ship". The Ellen F. McAllister was a very busy 1000 horsepower ship-docking tug that carried a docking master on board.

Our tug was the Peter B. McAllister, a canaler with a low silhouette and pilothouse to allow us to get under the bridges in the New York State barge canal system. The Peter B. had a low speed diesel engine that produced 750 horsepower. The Hurdy Gurdy was a 6 cylinder Superior auxiliary diesel that ran a 40 KW direct-current generator off one end and an air compressor through a PTO (power take-off) and clutch on the other end. I had no intention of starting it. That compressor was used if there was a lot of shifting and the main compressor that ran off the tail shaft on 5 big vee belts was not enough to keep up with the demand. I took great pride in being able to start and stop the main engine with very little air and had shifted barges many times without using it. The auxiliary was also very noisy. There was a shaft generator running off the main engine intermediate shaft by belts to make electricity whenever the main engine was running at more than dead slow. This gave us power and charged the batteries at the same time.

    I was only 21 years old and had just received my United States Coast Guard Engineers license and I thought I was the cat's meow, not to mention I knew everything about everything. Captain Vic rang the jingle again because I had not answered the jingle with one of my own which was what you did when you were ready. I didn't ring back because I wasn't ready and he knew this. Almost immediately after that he rang one bell on the gong, calling for half ahead. He knew I wasn't ready and was just busting my chops and trying to make me hurry. I finally got the pump back together and ran up the ladder on the port side to the upper engine room where the control stand, engine gauges and thermometers were. I hit the jingle with my hand to signal I was ready and he answered immediately with a gong and two jingles on the bells. This meant slow ahead. I pushed up the throttle that was a large brass handle shaped like an old emergency brake with a ratchet, halfway up and turned the start-stop wheel counterclockwise. This would shift the camshaft aft so the ahead running camshaft lobes were in position for the rocker rollers of the exhaust, start and fuel injector valves to be able to run in the ahead mode. A little more pressure in the same direction of the start-stop wheel opened the main air start valve and 150 PSI air was admitted to the pistons that were just past top dead center driving the pistons down and causing the engine to rotate and start. The trick was to give it just enough air to start without overdoing it and wasting the air. Once I knew the engine had caught, I would come back off the start detent that was spring loaded and move the fuel ratchet back to dead slow.

If Captain Vic wanted to have the engine run slower yet, I could pull back on another lever below the throttle and that would pull out the wedges between the injector tops and the injector rocker swivel until the engine was just barely running. Sometimes we pulled it back just a little too far and stalled the engine. This would mean a restart and that would use up more air, something I didn't want to do.

Captain Vic worked the stern off and gave one bell to stop. The strain came off the line and the deckhand Carl quickly threw the turns off the bitt and whipped it off the dock cleat as though the line was string. I didn't see this, I just knew the procedure and Carl was one of the best. From my station in the upper engine room I could look out to port pretty well and if I leaned out the door I could see to the forward and aft quarter bitts. Across the engine room was another Dutch door with the top half usually open and two port lights that gave me a somewhat limited view but it was enough to let me see what was going on around us and allow me to anticipate what we were up to.

Then ... two bells to go back. Unless we got a jingle for full, we always gave three quarter speed astern. Vic let her run astern for just under half a minute using the rudder to help her go the way he wanted. The rudder didn't do much going back under power but when he stopped me with another bell, the rudder pulled the stern a little more to port as we left the slip. Carl was going past the engine room door to get his after lines ready and he said to me "better get the Hurdy Gurdy going Robert (he and the other Norwegian's pronounced it, Row' bert). I watched the steering shafting overhead rotate as Vic turned the rudder to starboard and was anticipating the one bell and a jingle to bring us around to starboard. This, to clear the pier head and make for the next slip where the shifting was to take place. I had to force myself not to look at the gong hammer and make a false maneuver; Vic had a nervous habit of raising and lowering the hammer without actually causing the gong to ring. If you looked it might seem like he rang it and you could make a mistake. The tide and rudder carried us to where Vic was satisfied with his position and rang one bell and one jingle. As quick as I could I swung the start-stop wheel to the start position at the same time as I pushed up the throttle lever, the cam shifted, the engine rotated, a little sluggish at first as she overcame the astern way on the propeller when the flywheel brake released, then it quickly turned over and caught as I released the start-stop wheel and allowed it to come back to the run detent. I could have saved half a second if I shifted the cam before I got the bell but I didn't want to use the air moving the cam if Vic gave me another backing bell.

We went into the slip and made up to two deck barges, brought them around to the other side of the pier and landed them. Carl tied them off. I went aft and let the tugs stern line go as Carl let the headline go and held the towing strap until I got back in the engine room to answer Vic's two bells to go back. As soon as he got enough slack he snapped it off with little effort. We were going back to pick up the last two barges and Carl walked by again and said I had better start the Hurdy Gurdy. He and Vic both knew it wasn't running because you couldn't help but hear it when it was. I wasn't worried, I had pretty good air left and Vic wasn't giving me any extra bells on purpose to make me use more air. He did this occasionally to keep me humble.

Coming back to the pier where we were going to pick up the remaining barges, the pier head was on our portside giving me a great view from the operating stand. We turned hard to port to enter the slip and Captain Vic being the ace he was, used the tide to bring us close to the end of the pier and worked the tug up into the current at a full ahead bell to bring us towards the barges at the same time sliding west and making headway to our target. Beautiful. I had seen this many times and was ready. Vic always gave three bells and a jingle in close quarters coming from full ahead instead of the regulation four bells and a jingle but I was used to this and was all set and in the flow. I loved this. I was hanging out the engine room door watching as we got close and Vic rang the expected three bells and a jingle. Without really looking I reached in, pulled the throttle back, turned the directional wheel clockwise to stop, waited for what I felt to be the right amount of time and turned the wheel again to the astern start position. The timing was perfect I knew as I pushed the throttle lever up to three quarter speed. Boy, we were coming in fast. Too fast. Without waiting I reached in and pushed the throttle up a couple of clicks on the ratchet. I no sooner did this when I got another jingle from Vic. We were still coming in fast but at a shallow angle because Captain Vic was used to steamboats, direct drive diesels and engineers who answered bells wrong. I reached in and pushed the throttle all the way to the stop as I looked out in wonder. Why were we coming in so fast? Then I got the bells again, three bells and a jingle. Uh, oh, that meant start all over again as he wasn't getting what he wanted. This time I turned all the way around and looked into the engine room. Oh no! The upper engine room was filled with smoke. I quickly dropped the throttle to idle and the directional wheel to stop. That's when I realized what had happened. In my all knowing, wise guy, fast shifting mode I had not waited long enough at the stop position for the flywheel brake to slow the engine down enough when I first got the bells for full astern. Even though the cam had shifted, the engine and propeller were still rotating ahead. This allowed the engine to keep going in the ahead position using the exhaust valves as the intake and the intake valves as the exhaust. What a mess, I could hardly see through all the smoke. Carl was yelling "go back, go back Row' bert!" I could hear Captain Vic screaming and I was momentarily confused. Vic rang the same three bells and a jingle again. This got me back to my senses and I shifted the wheel to reverse, started the engine in the astern direction and gave her full throttle as fast as I could.

Well, I was just a little too late. We hit the closest barge with our port hip fender so hard we bounced off about ten feet. When you hit something that is not going to move with a tug that weighs about 100 tons at that rate of speed and all of a sudden shoot off in a different direction most of the loose stuff on board doesn't cooperate. Like the guys who were off watch in their bunks, the stores, the soup and the potatoes on the stove, the log books, pencils, coffee cups and other loose stuff that went flying. The cook came out of the galley screaming followed by a cloud of steam from the spilled soup and potato water on the hot surface of the oil stove. The other assistant engineer came running out of his bunkroom into the smoky engine room with raw fright in his eyes and his mouth wide open but no sound coming out, the off duty deckhand came up on deck from the foc's'le with a life jacket in his hand. Later, looking back I would laugh at the whole scene but at that moment I was embarrassed, scared, confused and praying that I hadn't damaged the engine. I had to hold my cool in front of Carl and Teddy, the assistant engineer, the cook was the least of my worries as he just kept babbling on about his potatoes but Captain Vic was another matter. Not only did he hold my future in his hands but I didn't want to feel like I failed in his eyes. I had gotten a bell to stop but I didn't get any after that and we were just drifting across the slip. Then I heard Vic walking down the deck. Uh oh, here comes the screaming. Vic stopped in front of the open engine room door and just looked at me with his hands on his hips and the slightest of smirks on his face, as if to say "What happened hot shot? You're not so sharp after all are you?" He then walked slowly back to the pilothouse and resumed the shifting. I started the Hurdy Gurdy.

The smoke soon cleared and the other Assistant Engineer was relieved to see there was no damage to the engine. He had never seen this happen before but I had, I had done it a couple of times when I was learning. It would never happen to Teddy though as he was not interested in being a fast shifter. It was almost time for the off watch to get up anyway but they all came around to the engine room door to razz me. The deckhand and the assistant helped the cook clean up and get everything back where it belonged. By the time Cookie rang the dinner bell, all was well.

We completed the shifting just before we were relieved and the other watch then helped the Ellen F. into the slip with her ship. We hung on (put a line out and shutdown) for about a half an hour and then got our orders over the VHF radio to help the Ellen F. out of a pier right near the mouth of the Gowanus Canal. It was going to be a light ship going to stream. The mate wasn't happy about this. He just did a docking job this morning but it was an easy one and in daylight. This would be a much harder job and now it was dark. The mate usually only worked in the NYS barge canal and stayed home for the winter season when the canal closed. We would probably make one more trip to the canal so he was still aboard. He tried to get out of the job but the dispatcher said we were the only boat around unless he hired an outside tug. Well, nobody wanted that to get out so he said okay. I went and sat on the stern hawser rack with my coffee and cigarette to watch. I also thought it would be a good idea to stay up until this job was over. The Docking Pilot told our mate to lay at the end of the pier and wait until he backed out of the slip. Then we were to get on the ships port forward quarter to help the Ellen F. push him West. In the meantime the Ellen F. was up in the slip at a ninety degree angle to the ship's bow. She would pinch the starboard bow in, which in turn would bring the ships stern off the pier and then the Pilot would have the ship come half astern. As the ship gained sternway and the Ellen F. lay all stopped, her line would become taut and pull her bow around towards the ship. At the same time because of the Ellen's weight the line also pulled the ship's bow away from the pier so it was all clear. With an ebb tide the pilot needed both tugs to get the bow going west quickly while he came full ahead on the ships propeller and a hard right rudder to make the turn in these very tight quarters. The Peter B. started to come up alongside the ship aft of the Ellen F. The ship was steam powered.

    Whenever a ship with this type of propulsion would first leave a pier in a cold state they could never give you more than 70 percent power, which didn't make the job any easier for the pilot. The Ellen F. now came ahead getting lined up for the tip of the port bow. As soon as the pilot thought he could clear the next pier head, he came ahead on the ship and blew his mouth whistle signaling the Ellen to come full ahead on the port bow and the ships whistle for us to do the same. The crew on the Ellen was experienced and they were in place and hooked up before you knew it. We, on the other hand, took time to jockey ourselves into position and when we did the ship was turning so fast and with some headway so we could not get as far forward as we should have and at no better angle than about 45 degrees. Between the two tugs and the ships propellers splashing and thumping away at 70 percent revolutions we were turning pretty fast. The splashing was because she was light and the propeller was not fully submerged. We did well though. Now with even more headway on the ship the pilot had both tugs go to one bell. We were almost flat against the ships side now and sliding back. We did not have a line out like the Ellen F. to hold us in place. The Pilot blew one long and two short on the ships whistle to signal us to let go or in this case to get away. The ship was still turning to starboard though and this was pushing her stern to port pressing us against the ship. We were still sliding back and couldn't peel off. The mate rang for full ahead and put the rudder over to port. This only put the port rail in the water and we were still sliding back.

Now you could see and hear the ships propeller getting closer. What you hear is more of a thump, thump, thump than a splash, splash, splash. If that propeller turning at that speed were to come in contact with our 3/8" steel hull it would slice right through it and keep slicing as it turned and we moved aft. No pump would ever keep up with the amount of water that would be coming in from the multiple slices and we would sink in five minutes.

The mate rang another jingle but I didn't feel much of a difference in engine vibration so I ran up the starboard side between us and the ship, the port side was not an option as the deck was under water. "Hook it up, hook it up" I yelled to Teddy. He shrugged and pointed to the throttle that was in the 85 percent position and Teddy had never had it past there. The mate tried to put the rudder to starboard now to bring our stern off as we were beginning to go under the stern counter of the ship towards the turning and thumping propeller.

It's funny how your perspective changes when circumstances get a little hairy. The area near the mouth of the Gowanus Canal looked very small and close at the start of the job but all of a sudden, in the dark, with few lights ashore and the deck lights of the tug limiting your far vision, the noise of the engine and the ships propeller, the black water of the harbor looked very large and foreboding in this dangerous situation.

Vic had gotten out his bunk in his underwear and took the wheel from the mate; he rang another jingle that almost pulled the cow bell off the overhead. Teddy just stood there not knowing what to do. I came in the engine room from the starboard side door and went under the shiny brass railing that went all around the top of the engine, stepped on a cylinder head while keeping my feet away from the intake and exhaust valves and the rocker arms that were pounding up and down, reached over the railing on the far side and grabbed the throttle handle. Teddy did not know what was happening and was confused so he didn't try to stop me as I pulled the lever to its limit. At around the same time or just before this Captain Vic blew the alarm on the tugs horn. Later, I remembered hearing it but at the time all I could think of was the thump, thump, thump of the approaching propeller. The Pilot, realizing what was happening made a very clever maneuver. Instead of stopping or slowing the ships wheel which by that time would have gobbled us up anyway, he turned the rudder hard to port moving the ships stern away from us and at the same time directing the wheel wash towards the Peter B.

The ships stern moving away, the tugs increase in engine speed and Captain Vic using the rudder just the right amount allowed us to peel off without too much rudder. If he came too hard to port we still would have gone under the stern counter and into the prop. We had just missed being sliced open and sunk.

Teddy who still had no idea of the danger we were in was only interested in getting the engine speed back to his idea of full. He was hearing noises he never heard before and vibrations he never felt before and just wanted things back to normal. I signaled okay and he slowed her down a little.

We went to a pier, tied off and shut down. Everyone congregated in the galley, sat down and had coffee. No one said much of anything for a long time. The satellite speaker in the galley was squawking "794 to the Peter B., 794 to the Peter B." but no one made an attempt to answer. After a while the mate said he was getting off in the morning and wouldn't be back until the spring season. Vic said in a low voice and without any anger that he thought it would probably be a good idea. Teddy said he was going to tell the chief when he came back that I made him speed up the engine more than he wanted to. The deck hand said he was going to get the lines ready because there was going to be a lot of coffee barge work tonight. The cook said he had to go get ready for bed if he was going to get up at 4:30 am.

And just like that, everything was back to normal.

## Chapter 31 - Runaway Tug

One time we were delivering a 20,000 barrel Gulf oil barge up to Rensselaer ,New York. After we dropped off the barge at the terminal we went to McAllister's tie up dock in Rensselaer. The engine crew that I was part of started to do some work on the engine and the auxiliaries. The cook was cleaning up from lunch in the galley and the deckhand who was off watch was in the forecastle making up his bunk. The mate had gone to bed. The other deckhand, Carl and the Capt. went up to the bowling alley close by to have a couple of beers. When our work was done the chief, the assistant and I went up to the town and did a little shopping for some personal necessities we needed on the boat. On the way back as we were about a block from the boat we heard engine signal bells ringing on the tug. Capt. Vic was signaling the engine room to start the engines and get underway. Vic we found out later had a fight with Carl and decided to leave him there and he stormed out of the bowling alley and went right to the boat. He then let all the lines go between the tug and the dock. He called up the engine room on the speaking tube and started ringing bells so we could get the engine going. Unfortunately all of us engine crew were still walking back from doing our shopping. The boat started drifting down the river and behind the boat and in its path was a Marina with many small boats tied to floating pontoons. We all started to run but we didn't know what to do.

I saw the boat was quite a ways away from the dock now, drifting down towards the Marina so when I got past the Runners house/office between it and the Marina there was an open field with some bushes and no path but I ran through it, jumped over a small fence to the Marina and ran down the dock. As I was running down the dock towards the floating pontoons I never thought I would make it. I thought that I would end up in the water and would have to swim to the boat which was not too far off the dock but still a ways for a running jump. It really didn't matter I was going to have to do it or allow the tug to go on drifting down the river and we all would've been in big trouble. When I ran to the end of the marina pontoons I jumped with all I had and I thought I would end up in the water but I ended up with my feet inside the tire of a tire fender and stuck my arms out and grabbed the waist rail. I pulled myself up and over and got into the engine room, opened the air valve and started the engine slow ahead. Vic then rang for half ahead and we got away from the Marina and made our way back to the tie up berth and the second deckhand who was in the forecastle with the cook came up to see what was going on and tied the boat up. We were all laughing at Vic and that made him all the madder but we got everything straightened out and went back to pick up the barge as if everything was normal, again.

# Chapter 32 - Some Other Stories

I was engineer on the John E. McAllister on the way to sail a ship out of Yonkers. A real nice day, just past the GW Bridge and I got a cup of coffee from the galley and went and sat on the after bitts and lit up a cigarette (we did that in those days!). All of a sudden I hear a bang and see a propeller fluke

shoot up in the air astern of us. Then the tug starts a dance. She was whipping her stern to port and starboard, but the Captain, Roy felt it right away and immediately slowed down. I ran up to the pilothouse and told him I just saw a fluke of the propeller fly off. "What! who are you bull shitting?" I'm telling you I saw the fluke fly up into the air, I said.

Okay, okay, let me call the office said Roy. "794, 794, the John E. to 794". Yeah, come in on the John E. "The chief says we just lost a fluke off the propeller" No answer for a few minutes and then, "Who are you trying to kid?". "Well, the chief said he saw it come off" said Roy. "Can you do this job?" Asked the dispatcher. No, we can't go above a slow bell was our answer. "Okay then, head back to the yard said the dispatcher, we will see if we can get you on dry dock right away, we need the boat". Next the Port engineer Eddie Quinn was on the radio asking how we knew we lost a fluke of the propeller, he didn't believe me either. So finally we got back to the yard, went on dry dock and low and behold, the fluke was missing. We changed out the wheel and went back to work that night.

That reminds me of the time I was on the Roderick McAllister and went to test the life boat davits and launching gear. I always got in trouble for this type of thing because they said I was afraid of sinking and drowning. I told them I was just safety conscious. I always checked out the fire extinguishers (usually past inspection date)and life jackets (some were rotten) also. Well, the rope falls were frozen and the line was rotted and parted. I got new rope falls and line from the yard after some trouble and begging. It was amazing how hard it was to get this stuff. It was as though if they gave it out they couldn't get more. When I finally got the material I

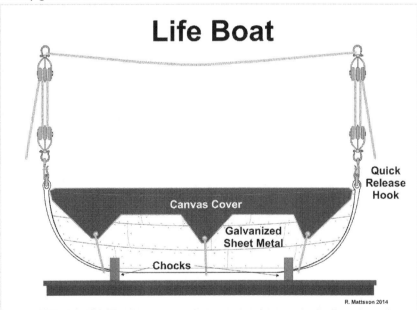

changed it all out. When it was all set up, I tried to pull the life boat up but it wouldn't budge. I got the deckhand and we tried again. Still no go, so we got the cook and the three of us pulled for all we were worth and finally the life boat broke free but the two bottom strakes of galvanized steel sheet at the keel of the lifeboat stayed on the chocks. They had been painted for so many years that the sheet metal was stuck to the chocks and the rivets and sheet metal were rusted from the inside. All of a sudden the crew realized how important this was. We were immediately given another old lifeboat to replace that one. Not long after this, the life boats were slowly removed and replaced with inflatable rafts.

Speaking of the Roderick, that reminds me of the time we were hanging on at the end of the 69th Street pier in Brooklyn. The Roderick like all the tugs with the LST running gear had a Marquette governor on the main engine. I thought I was pretty good at adjusting them as I had done a few before but I got a little deeper into this one than I should have. The chief had gotten off earlier as this was crew change day so when I got it back together and it wasn't working there was no one to help me. Sure enough I got a jingle to get her up and running. I ran up to the captain in the pilot house and told him my problem. I didn't want anyone to find out I screwed up and was panicky. The captain asked if I knew the bell system. I told him yes but the engine controls were about 18' from the reversing controls so we wouldn't be able to shift and change speed quickly. He said it wasn't a problem, he would let the pilot know and we could be the stern boat. I was relieved but nervous as we left the pier and made our way to the ship job. I got very few bells as the captain and pilot were working with me and the ship was docked without a problem. Although I was exhausted from running back an forth from the front of the main engine to the back of the reduction gear where the manual shifting arm was. When we got back to 69th Street the captain asked the chief from the Ellen F. McAllister to come over and help me. He did and showed me where I went wrong and we got it running again. I was very careful after that.

# Chapter 33 - Stranded on Ice Flows

I have (as many have) worked the tugs in 0 degree weather, dry docks in 0 degree weather, the end of the piers in the shipyard with heavy wind and many other places where the cold was unbearable. I have been stuck in the

ice in the Hudson, (and changed crew on the ice) but the toughest in my opinion is working on the deck of an oil barge, repairing the pump or pump engines in the anchorage in the single digits with the wind blowing hard and the cargo cooling and the (warm) office and ship's crew and agent continually asking when you will be done! Sometimes I wondered if I had fingers left. That said, once we got everything going again it was a great feeling. Hot coffee was better than a martini at that point. A tough job on the older tugs was running in the ice on the Hudson River with a tug that had sea chests and no recirculating lines. Every five minutes the duplex strainer would plug up with slush ice and I had to switch over to the one I just cleaned and pull the one with ice slush in it out with my hands. My hands didn't even get cold, they went right to extreme pain. I would bang it a few times on the 6" sea water piping and then hose it out and stick it back in to get ready for the other side to plug up. This could go on for hours. It was so much easier if the tug had a ballast tank we could recirculate to and from or even better, keel coolers or Kort nozzle coolers like the Brian A. McAllister.

Attached are some of my ice pictures from January, 1963. We rescued a deer and three dogs while southbound on the Hudson River off Poughkeepsie with the Brian A. McAllister pushing a light oil barge. The dogs had chased the deer out on the ice and they were all stranded on the ice floes. I had to go into ice water thigh deep from a ladder tied to the waist railing to grab them as the captain would back down on them. Once we got the dogs and the deer on board the dogs wanted to get at the deer and we had to put them in the foc's'le. We also had to hog tie the doe so she wouldn't' run around the deck and try to kick us. We tied up at the Newburgh, N.Y. city dock and called the authorities. A police detective arrived first and asked if we could race the engine so the noise would mask his shot as he killed the deer. We went nuts and said "no way, not after what we went through to save her". He relented and called the animal control people and a real nice young game warden came onboard a little later that night. The ASPCA had already taken the dogs off. He got the Doe into his van with our help and left. In the meantime a real heavy snowstorm prevented us from leaving that night or the next day. The following morning he came down to the pier and told us his wife and daughter were feeding the doe from their hands. He said they would release her to the wild in about a week. We all received citation certificates from the Newburg Society for the Prevention of Cruelty to Animals.

DATE January 30, 1963

Mr. Robert Mattson
NAME

Gulfport, Staten Island, N. Y.
ADDRESS

*In appreciation of your act of kindness to dumb creatures, we issue this*

# Citation of Honor

*and commend and extol you as a co-worker in the cause of humane work.*

**Newburgh Society for the Prevention of Cruelty to Animals**

*Albert Seeger MacDowell*
President

*Mary H. Smith*
Corresponding Sec'y.

## Chapter 34 - Christine E. Fire

This story is a decade (1979) or more later than the previous tales but I thought I would throw it in. There are many stories between this and the others but I wanted to get it down on paper before I forgot and who knows if I will ever write another *epic* like this one. As the marine superintendent I was called out in the wee hours of the morning and told I would have to go up to Haverstraw Bay where the Christine E. was burning out of control and was still in the notch of the Nepco 140. The last cargo was crude oil so her chance of blowing up if the fire reached her was high. The Helen McAllister was waiting for me at Dock 19 Jersey City where she was loading wrecking pumps. It seemed like forever to get to Haverstraw Bay after we left Jersey City and were on the radio with the office and the boats already on the scene the whole time. In the meantime the USCG Cutter Mahoney was hosing the tug down. When we got there she was pretty well gutted but no one wanted to go near her as she was still attached with her pushing cables in the notch of the barge and flames were coming out of the house. The crew had been taken off by Eugenia Moran and the barge had her anchor out. At 2:30 AM on the 26th we were informed by the Mahoney that they were hosing down the Christine E. and that most of the visible flames were gone and that clouds of steam are rising up from their efforts. They were also requesting a cutting torch. We arrived at the scene at 2:40 AM and came alongside the starboard stern of the Christine E. with the stern of the Helen. The heat was fairly intense but I climbed over with the torch and began to cut the cables.

If you have ever cut steel cables with a torch, you know you don't really cut as much as you melt the strands away. I had it done by 3:00 AM and we pulled the tug free. The Helen, Alexandra and the Mahoney were all spraying water on the tug. We determined there was a severe fire still burning in the lower forward engine room, slightly to starboard. We were spraying water, fog and foam into the engine room but it wasn't helping. I could tell the tug was sinking and said I wanted to ground her. The Coast Guard and Captain Duffy, V.P. of Operations of McAllister at the time, weren't so sure about that but we called New York and they said they would talk to A.J. McAllister Jr. By now the welds under the deck were breaking with force and loud noises. I told Captain Duffy I wanted to flood the engine room and again he called New York at 5:00 AM and A.J. McAllister Jr. said if that's what Bob recommends, then do it. The Mahoning and Alexandra beached her at Croton Point at 5:30 AM and none too soon as the after deck was even with the water. The Mahoney ran out of foam so we tried fog and water again. The Timothy McAllister went to Bowline Point to get more foam and returned at 9:30.

    The Croton Volunteer Fire Department with Fire Chief, Rick Sperano came on board and with gas powered cutting tools and they cut an opening in the port and starboard decks over the forward engine room at 12:45 PM. We put foam into these openings but it was no help. Captain Duffy borrowed an oxygen breathing apparatus from the firemen and made it part way down the engine room ladder. The heat drove him back but he saw that the fuel oil manifold on the bulkhead had ruptured and the manhole cover on the starboard fuel tank was also pissing out a stream. These were acting like oil burner nozzles. I was now trying to force water into the starboard fuel oil tank through the vent on deck but the deck was so hot I had to keep hopping from one foot to the other. The crew on the Alexandra noticed my dilemma and started to spray water on the deck from their fire hose. When the water hit the deck it turned to steam and it felt like someone stuck socks in my mouth and nose! I absolutely could not breath and had to blindly back down the deck. Two of the volunteer firemen went into the engine room with their OBA's and tried to foam the area with new foam delivered via USCG helicopter but still couldn't bring it under control. So at 2:00 PM we reversed the pumps and brought the water up to the upper engine room gratings at 3:00 PM.

The water and oil was still burning but we quickly put it out with foam at 3:15. A sigh of relief from everybody and then we reversed the pumps again at 3:30. I doubt if we would have been allowed to do that in this day and age. Anyway, we pumped it down to just below the floor plates and went in to see what was going on . With the help of the crew from the Alexandra we hosed down the upper PH, second deck and main deck. All cooled down, we left for Tug & Barge at 10:40 PM under tow of the Alexandra McAllister. The fire had been most severe at the starboard forward engine room. We found a plastic fuel tank sight glass melted and pouring out fuel, a fuel level sensor split and sending out a five finger stream of fuel

and the fuel oil tank manhole at floor plate level leaking a stream through the gasket at the bottom. I turned off all fuel valves and started to drain the main engines, generator engines and the hydraulic steering tanks and pumps.

When we got underway the tail shafts started to turn from being towed through the water. I didn't want this because the reduction gears were full of water. So I had the Alexandra stop, rig up an air hose to pass over to me and I put air on both the clutches on both engines. This locked the gears up and stopped the tail shafts from turning. I tightened both stern glands, got something to eat on the Alex and arrived at Tug & Barge, Dock 19, Jersey City at 2:30 AM on the 27th. I was tired, dirty and smelled like fire. My notes don't say what I did after that but I think I went home about noon.

## About the Author

Mr. Mattsson was employed in the New York Harbor Marine Industry for 57 years. He spent his younger years in the shipyard and on canal, harbor and coastwise tug boats. He sat before the USCG Examiner in 1961 and passed, receiving the first issue of his Engineers license. At the time he was employed by McAllister Towing of New York as an oiler. He then went on to become an Assistant Engineer, Chief Engineer, Port Engineer, Marine Superintendent and General Manager of their shipyard, Tug & Barge Dry Docks, Inc. During his time off when he was a tug engineer he worked in the shipyard as a First Class Outside Machinist.

Mr. Mattsson was General Manager of Tug & Barge Dry Docks and instrumental in moving the entire shipyard and its dry docks from Dock 19, Jersey City to a site at Pavonia Avenue, Jersey City in 1974 to make way for Liberty State Park. When that property was taken over by Jersey City in an Eminent Domain action in 1979, Mr. Mattsson left McAllister for Circle Line Sightseeing Company as their Marine Superintendent and Shipyard Manager in Mill Basin, Brooklyn, NY and quickly moved to the position of Senior Vice President of Operations at their 42nd Street, Manhattan, facility.

In 1984 Mr. Mattsson left Circle Line to become the Marine Superintendent for the Eklof Marine Corp. in Mariners Harbor, Staten Island, New York. After a short period Mr. Mattsson was promoted to Vice President of Operations and Consultant to their affiliate, Clean Water of New York. Eklof Marine Corp. was bought out by management employees and an investment group to become K-Sea Transportation Corp. in 1999. In 2003 K-Sea went public on the New York Stock Exchange and Mr. Mattsson then became the Executive Vice President and held that position until his retirement in 2005.

    Mr. Mattsson has been married to his beautiful wife Gail, since 1961, has a son, Shawn, married to Christine and has two lovely granddaughters, Samantha and Kara.

    At the present time he does consulting , web sites and graphics for Kirby Offshore Marine, Clean Water of New York and United Maintenance Corp. He also does a maintenance article once a month for his community newsletter. In his spare time he does graphics for his friends at tugboats@yahoo.com , and the Lord Nelson Victory Tugs Group. He also builds tug models from scratch and has a web site at www.bellboatbob.com. Twice a week he has fun making believe he is a golfer.

    He has also published an eBook of his graphics available at Amazon. The title is 'Tug Boat Graphics & Illustrations'.

Made in the USA
Charleston, SC
11 December 2014